To My Friends

To My Friends

MESSAGES OF COUNSEL
AND COMFORT

JEFFREY R. HOLLAND

DESERET
BOOK

SALT LAKE CITY, UTAH

Visit us at DeseretBook.com

Library of Congress Cataloging-in-Publication Data

(CIP data on file)
ISBN 978-1-62972-029-6

Printed in the United States of America
Publishers Printing, Salt Lake City, UT

10 9 8 7 6 5 4 3 2 1

Contents

A friend may well be the
masterpiece of creation.

—RALPH WALDO EMERSON

AFTER AN ENCOUNTER WITH

THE LIVING
SON

OF THE LIVING GOD,

 nothing is ever again

to be as it was before.

To my friends
who love the Lord

CHAPTER 1

THE FIRST GREAT COMMANDMENT

There is almost no group in history for whom I have more sympathy than I have for the eleven remaining Apostles immediately following the death of the Savior of the world. I think we sometimes forget just how inexperienced they still were and how totally dependent upon Jesus they had of necessity been. To them He had said, "Have I been so long time with you, and yet hast thou not known me . . . ?"[1]

But, of course, to them He hadn't been with them nearly long enough. Three years isn't long to call an entire Quorum of Twelve Apostles from a handful of new converts, purge from them the error of old ways, teach them the wonders of the gospel of Jesus Christ, and then leave them to carry on the work until they too were killed. Quite a staggering prospect for a group of newly ordained elders.

Especially the part about being left alone. Repeatedly Jesus had tried to tell them He was *not* going to remain physically present with them, but they either could not or would not comprehend such a wrenching thought. Mark writes:

"He taught his disciples, and said unto them, The Son of man is delivered into the hands of men, and they shall kill him; and after that he is killed, he shall rise the third day.

"But they understood not that saying, and were afraid to ask him."[2]

Then, after such a short time to learn and even less time to prepare, the unthinkable happened, the unbelievable was true. Their Lord and Master, their Counselor and King, was crucified. His mortal ministry was over, and the struggling little Church He had established seemed doomed to scorn and destined for extinction. His Apostles did witness Him in His resurrected state, but that only added to their bewilderment. As they surely must have wondered, "What do we do now?" they turned for an answer to Peter, the senior Apostle.

Here I ask your indulgence as I take some nonscriptural liberty in my portrayal of this exchange. In effect, Peter said to his associates: "Brethren, it has been a glorious three years. None of us could have imagined such a few short months ago the miracles we have seen and the divinity we have enjoyed. We have talked with, prayed with, and labored with the very Son of God Himself. We have walked with Him and wept with Him, and on the night of that horrible ending, no one wept more bitterly than I. But that is over. He has finished His work, and He has risen from the tomb. He has worked out His salvation and ours. So you ask, 'What do we do now?' I don't know more to tell you than to return to your former life, rejoicing. I intend to 'go a fishing.'" And at least six of the ten other remaining Apostles said in agreement, "We also go with thee." John, who was one of them, writes, "They went forth, and entered into a ship immediately."[3]

But, alas, the fishing wasn't very good. Their first night back on the lake, they caught nothing—not a single fish. With the first rays of dawn, they disappointedly turned toward the shore, where they saw in the distance a figure who called out to them, "Children, have you caught anything?" Glumly these Apostles-turned-again-fishermen gave the answer no fisherman wants to give. "We have caught nothing," they muttered, and to add insult to injury, they were being called "children."[4]

"Cast the net on the right side of the ship, and ye shall find,"[5] the stranger calls out—and with those simple words, recognition begins to flood over them. Just three years earlier these very men had been fishing on this very sea. On that occasion too they had "toiled all the night, and [had] taken nothing,"[6] the scripture says. But a fellow Galilean on the shore had called out to them to let down their nets, and they drew "a great multitude of fishes,"[7] enough that their nets broke, the catch filling two boats so heavily they had begun to sink.

Now it was happening again. These "children," as they

were rightly called, eagerly lowered their net, and "they were not able to draw it for the multitude of fishes."[8] John said the obvious: "It is the Lord."[9] And over the edge of the boat, the irrepressible Peter leaped.

After a joyful reunion with the resurrected Jesus, Peter had an exchange with the Savior that I consider the crucial turning point of the apostolic ministry generally and certainly for Peter personally, moving this great rock of a man to a majestic life of devoted service and leadership. Looking at their battered little boats, their frayed nets, and a stunning pile of 153 fish, Jesus said to His senior Apostle, "Peter, do you love me more than you love all this?" Peter said, "Yea, Lord; thou knowest that I love thee."[10]

The Savior responds to that reply but continues to look into the eyes of His disciple and says again, "Peter, do you love me?" Undoubtedly confused a bit by the repetition of the question, the great fisherman answers a second time, "Yea, Lord; thou knowest that I love thee."[11]

The Savior again gives a brief response, but with relentless scrutiny He asks for the third time, "Peter, do you love me?" By now surely Peter is feeling truly uncomfortable. Perhaps there is in his heart the memory of only a few days earlier when he had been asked another question three times and he had answered equally emphatically—but in the negative. Or perhaps he began to wonder if he misunderstood the Master Teacher's question. Or perhaps he was searching his heart, seeking honest confirmation of the answer he had given so readily, almost automatically. Whatever his feelings, Peter said for the third time, "Lord, . . . thou knowest that I love thee."[12]

To which Jesus responded (and here again I acknowledge my nonscriptural elaboration), perhaps saying something like: "Then Peter, why are you here? Why are we back on this same shore, by these same nets, having this same conversation? Wasn't it obvious then and isn't it obvious now that if I want fish, I can get fish? What I need, Peter, are disciples—and I need them forever. I need someone to feed my sheep and save my lambs. I need someone to preach my gospel and defend my faith. I need someone who loves me, truly, truly loves me, and loves what our Father in Heaven has commissioned me to do. Ours is not a feeble message. It is not a fleeting task. It is not hapless; it is not hopeless; it is not to be consigned to the ash heap of history. It is the work of Almighty God, and it is to change the world. So, Peter, for the second and presumably the last time, I am asking you to leave all this and to go teach and testify, labor and serve loyally until the day in which they will do to you exactly what they did to me."

Then, turning to all the Apostles, He might well have said something like: "Were you as foolhardy as the scribes and Pharisees? As Herod and Pilate? Did you, like they, think that this work could be killed simply by killing me? Did you, like they, think the cross and the nails and the tomb were the end of it all and each could blissfully go back to being whatever you were before? Children, did not my life and my love touch your hearts more deeply than this?"

I am not certain just what our experience will be on Judgment Day, but I will be very surprised if at some point in that conversation, God does not ask us exactly what Christ asked Peter: "Did you love me?" I think He will want to know if in our very mortal, very inadequate, and sometimes childish grasp of things, did we at least understand *one* commandment, the first and greatest commandment of them all—"Thou shalt love the Lord thy God with all thy heart, and with all thy soul, and with all thy strength, and with all thy mind."[13] And if at such a moment we can stammer out, "Yea, Lord, thou knowest that I love thee," then He may remind us that the crowning characteristic of love is always loyalty.

"If ye love me, keep my commandments,"[14] Jesus said. So we have neighbors to bless, children to protect, the poor to lift up, and the truth to defend. We have wrongs to make right, truths to share, and good to do. In short, we have a life of devoted discipleship to give in demonstrating our love of the Lord. We can't quit and we can't go back. After an encounter with the living Son of the living God, nothing is ever again to be as it was before. The Crucifixion, Atonement, and Resurrection of Jesus Christ mark the beginning of a Christian life, not the end of it. It was this truth, this reality, that allowed a handful of Galilean fishermen-turned-again-Apostles without "a single synagogue or sword"[15] to leave those nets a second time and go on to shape the history of the world in which we now live.

I testify from the bottom of my heart, with the intensity

of my soul, that those apostolic keys have been restored to the earth, and they are found in The Church of Jesus Christ of Latter-day Saints. To those who have not yet joined with us in this great final cause of Christ, we say, "Please come." To those who were once with us but have retreated, preferring to pick and choose a few cultural hors d'oeuvres from the smorgasbord of the Restoration and leave the rest of the feast, I say that I fear you face a lot of long nights and empty nets. The call is to come back, to stay true, to love God, and to lend a hand. I include in that call to fixed faithfulness every returned missionary who ever stood in a baptismal font and with arm to the square said, "Having been commissioned of Jesus Christ."[16] That commission was to have changed your convert forever, but it was surely supposed to have changed you forever as well. To the youth of the Church rising up to missions and temples and marriage, we say: "Love God and remain clean from the blood and sins of this generation. You have a monumental work to do. Your Father in Heaven expects your loyalty and your love at every stage of your life."

The voice of Christ comes ringing down through the halls of time, asking each one of us while there is time, "Do you love me?" And for every one of us, I answer with my honor and my soul, "Yea, Lord, we do love thee." And having set our "hand to the plough,"[17] we will never look back until this work is finished and love of God and neighbor rules the world.

NOTES

From a talk given at general conference, October 2012.

1. John 14:9.
2. Mark 9:31–32.
3. John 21:3.
4. See John 21:5.
5. John 21:6.
6. Luke 5:5.
7. Luke 5:6.
8. John 21:6.
9. John 21:7.
10. John 21:15.
11. John 21:16.
12. John 21:17.
13. Luke 10:27; see also Matthew 22:37–38.
14. John 14:15.
15. Frederic W. Farrar, *The Life of Christ* (1994), 656; see chapter 62 for more on the plight of this newly founded Church.
16. Doctrine and Covenants 20:73.
17. Luke 9:62.

WE ALL HAVE NEED TO REPENT,
AND WE ALL HAVE THE OBLIGATION
TO FORGIVE. TRUE FRIENDS,
MAGNANIMOUS FRIENDS, GENUINE
LATTER-DAY SAINT FRIENDS WILL
HELP EACH OTHER DO THAT.

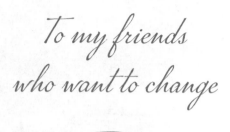

To my friends who want to change

CHAPTER 2

"IF MY FRIENDS WILL HELP ME"

As you might suppose, in the course of more than a quarter century as a General Authority, I have met, spoken with, and sometimes had to interview hundreds of people who have had problems—people who have struggled or are sorrowful or who feel blocked in their progress because of a transgression in their lives. The purpose of those visits and interviews has always been to lift that burden from their lives.

If you need a burden lifted, I want you to imagine I am in a personal, private, closed-door chat with you. I want to help you if I can.

First of all, don't feel abandoned or forsaken or forever damaged if you have made a mistake, even a serious mistake.

Everyone has, with some mistakes of course being more serious than others. But as the Apostle Paul knew personally, "*All* have sinned, and come short of the glory of God."[1]

As much as our Father in Heaven has warned against sin and continually pleads against committing it, He nevertheless knew, clear back in the premortal councils of heaven, that we wouldn't do everything right. So He planned for and promised a way out of our problems, described in the scriptures as "*the* way." That way out of our problems, "the way, the truth, and the life,"[2] is the Atonement of His perfect, totally obedient Son—the only one in the entire family who would *not* transgress when He came to earth. Only that Son was worthy enough and therefore capable of lifting our sins from our shoulders and putting them on His.

We shouted for joy at that offer of help, and from that moment on we loved Christ (or certainly should have) because He first loved us. But to take full advantage of the Atonement and obtain forgiveness of those sins, we do have to do some very basic things. We *do* owe something for this gift. We must have faith in Christ and believe in His redeeming power. We must be honest about our mistakes—confront them, confess them, truly regret them, and forsake them. Then we must vow honestly to live as much like Christ as we possibly can, including following Him in the saving ordinances of the gospel.

But there are two common problems in all of this: We don't believe we can repent and change, or else we don't believe we can be forgiven and have that guilt lifted even if we do change. Let's talk about those erroneous assumptions.

First, let's address the fear that we can't change, can't stop making those mistakes, partly because we have tried in the past and failed.

There is only one person in the universe who wants you to believe that you cannot change or improve your life and that you should give up trying. That is the impish fellow in charge of shoveling coal down in the netherworld of outer darkness. There is a devil, he is real, and he is the only one—plus some of his benighted minions—who wants you to think you can't change. Of course you can change. That is the plan of God. It was conceived by the Father and implemented by the Son, much to the dismay of Lucifer, who wanted so much to make sure that no one changed or improved—ever, in any way. If we feel we cannot repent, cannot change, that we are some kind of robot from a science-fiction movie who has no voli-tion, no will, no concept of good, no access to or belief in the Atonement, which is the agent for all desirable and righteous change—if we think that we are such hapless victims, such rag-doll, pathetic, hollow beings, then we *are* being led "carefully down to hell,"[3] as Nephi says of the devil's tactics in the Book of Mormon.

I am not sure what your most serious sins are. Some may be sexual and among the most serious God Himself has de-cried. Others may be less serious but still wrong. Whatever the list, it's bound to be long when we add up all the dumb things we've done or said or been. And my greatest fear is that you will not believe you can escape from them, that you are convinced your guilt and your continuing mistakes will go on forever. This is a debilitating outlook to have and it can make you sick in your soul. Let me give you a famous example of the impact of such guilt.

We watch Shakespeare's Macbeth—cousin of the king, masterful, strong, honored and honorable—descend through a horrible series of bloody deeds by which his very soul is increasingly "tortured by an agony which [knows no] . . . repose."[4] Shapes of terror appear before his eyes, and the sounds of hell clamor in his ears.

His wife and co-conspirator goes mad with the strain, and her guilty heart and tormented conscience rend her days and terrify his nights so incessantly that Macbeth says to his physician:

> *Canst thou not minister to a mind diseased,*
> *Pluck from the memory a rooted sorrow,*
> *Raze out the written troubles of the brain*
> *And with some sweet oblivious antidote*
> *Cleanse the stuff'd bosom of that perilous stuff*
> *Which weighs upon the heart?*[5]

The doctor shakes his head over such diseases of the soul and says:

> *Therein the patient*
> *Must minister to himself.*[6]

But the anguish continues unabated until Macbeth says on the day he will die:

> *Out, out, brief candle!*
> *Life's but a walking shadow, a poor player*
> *That struts and frets his hour upon the stage*
> *And then is heard no more: it is a tale*
> *Told by an idiot, full of sound and fury,*
> *Signifying nothing.*[7]

Macbeth's murders are sins too strong for the kind of transgression you and I should need to discuss. But I believe the despair of his final hopelessness can be applied at least in part to our own circumstances. Unless we believe in repentance and restoration, unless we believe there can be a way back from our mistakes, unless we believe we can progress on solid ground with our past put behind us and genuine hope for the future— then I think we in our own way are as hopeless as Macbeth, and our view of life is just as depressing. It is entirely possible that our sins can so depress us that we *do* become shadows, feeble players on a perverse stage, in a tale told by an idiot. And unfortunately, in such a burdened state, we are the idiots.

Of the book he would call *The Miracle of Forgiveness,* President Spencer W. Kimball said:

"This book indicates the seriousness of breaking God's commandments; shows that sin can bring only sorrow, remorse, disappointment, and anguish; and warns that the small indiscretions evolve into larger ones and finally into major transgressions which bring heavy penalties. . . .

"[But] having come to recognize their deep sin, many have tended to surrender hope, not having a clear knowledge of the scriptures and of the redeeming power of Christ.

"[So I also] write to make the joyous affirmation that man can be literally transformed by his own repentance and by God's gift of forgiveness. . . .

"It is my humble hope that . . . [those] who are suffering the baleful effects of sin may be helped to find the way from darkness to light, from suffering to peace, from misery to hope, and from spiritual death to eternal life."[8]

That is what I want for you. Without ever minimizing the seriousness of our mistakes, I want you to believe that Jesus Christ gives us a way back. *We must believe* in movement "from darkness to light, from suffering to peace, from misery to hope."[9]

What if Alma had not come back? He had made serious mistakes, more serious perhaps than we know. He is described as "a very wicked and an idolatrous man,"[10] one who sought to "destroy the church"[11] and who delighted in rebelling against God. He was, in short, "the very vilest of sinners."[12] The strongest denunciation came from his own lips when he said to his son Helaman, "I had rebelled against my God. . . . I had murdered many of his children, or rather led them away unto destruction; . . . so great had been my iniquities, that the very thought of coming into the presence of my God did rack my soul with inexpressible horror."[13]

He may not have been Macbeth, but that is a frightening

description of a man's standing before God. But he came back. Not without anguish and suffering and fear, not without "wading through much tribulation, repenting nigh unto death."[14] But he paid the full price and came back on the strength of Christ's love. And every life thereafter, both in the Book of Mormon itself and in our generation, has been enriched because of the life Alma then lived.

What if mistakes had so crippled Peter that he had not come back, stronger than ever, after the Crucifixion and Resurrection of the Master? Several years ago President Gordon B. Hinckley spoke of Peter's struggle. After recounting the events of Jesus's ordeal in accusations, mock trials, and imprisonment, and Peter's remorseful acquiescence to it, he said:

"As I have read this account my heart goes out to Peter. So many of us are so much like him. We pledge our loyalty; we affirm our determination to be of good courage; we declare, sometimes even publicly, that come what may we will do the right thing, that we will stand for the right cause, that we will be true to ourselves and to others.

"Then the pressures begin to build. Sometimes these are social pressures. Sometimes they are personal appetites. Sometimes they are false ambitions. There is a weakening of the will. There is a softening of discipline. There is capitulation. And then there is remorse, self-accusation, and bitter tears of regret."[15]

Well, if Peter's story were to have ended there, with him

cursing and swearing and saying, "I know not the man," surely it would be among the most pathetic in all scripture.

But Peter came back.

He squared his shoulders and stiffened his resolve and made up for lost ground. He took command of a frightened little band of Church members. He preached such a moving sermon on the day of Pentecost that three thousand in the audience applied for baptism. Days later, five thousand heard him and were baptized. Faith in Peter's faith brought the sick into the streets on their beds of affliction "that at the least the shadow of Peter passing by might overshadow some of them."[16] He fearlessly spoke for his brethren when they were arraigned before the Sanhedrin and when they were cast into prison. He entertained angels and received the vision that led to carrying the gospel to the Gentiles. He became in every sense the rock Christ promised he would be. Of such a life President Hinckley said:

"I pray that you may draw comfort and resolution from the example of Peter who, though he had walked daily with Jesus, in an hour of extremity denied both the Lord and the testimony which he carried in his own heart. But he rose above this, and became a mighty defender and a powerful advocate. So too, there is a way for you to turn about and . . . [build] the kingdom of God."[17]

Let me say now a word about the other doubt we have— the fear that even if we change, we won't be forgiven of our sins and mistakes in life, therefore the damage has been done and change means nothing. First of all, let me readily admit we sometimes feel this way because others—ironically, those we call our friends—won't let us feel we can be forgiven.

I grew up in the same town as a boy who had no father and precious few of the other blessings of life. The young men in our community found it easy to tease and taunt and bully him. And in the process of it all, he made some mistakes. He began to drink and smoke, and gospel principles that had never meant much to him now meant almost nothing. He had been cast in a role by LDS friends who should have known better, and he began to play the part perfectly. Soon he drank even more, went to school even less, and went to church not at all. Then one day he was gone. Some said they thought he had joined the army.

Fifteen or sixteen years later he came back home. At least, he tried to come home. He had found the significance of the gospel in his life. He had married a wonderful girl, and they had a family. But he discovered something upon his return. He had changed, but some of his old friends hadn't—and they were unwilling to let him escape his past.

This was hard for him and hard for his family. Eventually they moved away. For reasons that don't need to be detailed here, the story goes on to a very unhappy ending. He died just a few years later, in his early forties. That's too young to die these days, and it's certainly too young to die when true friends, forgiving friends, could have helped you live.

When a battered, weary swimmer tries to get back to shore

after having fought strong winds and rough waves that he should never have challenged in the first place, those of us who might have had better judgment, or perhaps just better luck, ought not to row out to his side, beat him with our oars, and shove his head back underwater. That's not what boats were made for. But some of us do that to each other.

Even if we admit our errors, confess them, and want to repent, want to change, *can we be forgiven?* The answer is yes, yes, yes! That is what the Atonement of Jesus Christ is all about. Let me share one of the sweetest stories of forgiveness in the history of this Church.

In the early years of the developing Church, the Prophet Joseph Smith had no more faithful aide than William Wines Phelps. Brother Phelps, a former newspaper editor, had joined the Church in Kirtland and was of such assistance to those early leaders that they sent him as one of the first Latter-day Saints to the New Jerusalem—Jackson County, Missouri. There he was called by the Lord to the stake presidency of that "center stake of Zion."

But then troubles developed. At first they were largely ecclesiastical aberrations, but then there were financial improprieties. Things became so serious that the Lord revealed to Joseph Smith that if Phelps did not repent, he would be "removed out of [his] place."[18] He did not repent and was excommunicated on March 10, 1838.

The Prophet Joseph and others immediately tried to love Phelps back into the fold, but he would have nothing of it.

Then in the fall of that violent year W. W. Phelps, along with others, signed a deadly, damaging affidavit against the Prophet and other leaders of the Church, personally pointing them out in a public setting, thereby identifying them for arrest by local officers of the law. The result was that Joseph Smith was sentenced to be executed on the town square in Far West, Missouri, Friday morning, November 2, 1838. Through the monumental courage of General Alexander Doniphan, the Prophet was miraculously spared the execution Phelps and others had precipitated, but he was not spared spending five months—November through April—in several Missouri prisons, the most noted of which was the pit known ironically as Liberty Jail.

I do not need to recount for you the suffering of the Saints through that period. The anguish of those not captive was in many ways more severe than that of those imprisoned. The persecution intensified until the Saints sought yet again to find refuge from the storm. With Joseph in chains, praying for their safety and giving some direction by letter, they made their way toward Commerce, Illinois, a malarial swamp on the Mississippi River where they would try once more to build the city of Zion. And so much of this travail, this torment and heartache, was due to men of their own brotherhood like W. W. Phelps.

But we're speaking here of change and repentance, of forgiveness and happy endings, and this story has one. Two very difficult years later, with wrenching anguish and remorse of conscience, Phelps wrote to Joseph Smith in Nauvoo.

"Brother Joseph: . . . I am as the prodigal son. . . . I have seen the folly of my way, and I tremble at the gulf I have passed. . . . [I] ask my old brethren to forgive me, and though they chasten me to death, yet I will die with them, for their God is my God. The least place with them is enough for me, yea, it is bigger and better than all Babylon. . . .

"I know my situation, you know it, and God knows it, and *I want to be saved if my friends will help me.* . . . I have done wrong and I am sorry. . . . I ask forgiveness. . . . I want your fellowship; if you cannot grant that, grant me your peace and friendship, for we are brethren, and our communion used to be sweet."[19]

In an instant the Prophet wrote back. I know of no private document or personal response in the life of Joseph Smith—or anyone else, for that matter—that so powerfully demonstrates the magnificence of his soul. There is a lesson here for every one of us who claims to be a disciple of Christ.

He wrote:

"Dear Brother Phelps: . . . You may in some measure realize what my feelings . . . were when we read your letter. . . .

"We have suffered much in consequence of your behavior—the cup of gall, already full enough for mortals to drink, was indeed filled to overflowing when you turned against us. . . .

"However, the cup has been drunk, the will of our Father

has been done, and we are yet alive, for which we thank the Lord. And having been delivered from the hands of wicked men by the mercy of our God, we say it is your privilege to be delivered from the powers of the adversary, be brought into the liberty of God's dear children, and again take your stand among the Saints of the Most High. . . .

"Believing your confession to be real, and your repentance genuine, I shall be happy once again to give you the right hand of fellowship, and rejoice over the returning prodigal.

"'Come on, dear brother, since the war is past, For friends at first, are friends again at last.'

"Yours as ever, Joseph Smith, Jun."[20]

What an expression! What magnanimity of heart! That little letter is one of the many evidences in this Church of the inspired service and noble character of Joseph Smith. It only adds to the poignance of this invitation to Brother Phelps that exactly four years later—almost to the day—it would be W. W. Phelps who would be selected to preach Joseph Smith's funeral sermon in that terribly tense and emotional circumstance. Furthermore it would be W. W. Phelps who would memorialize the Prophet after the martyrdom at Carthage with his hymn of adoration, "Praise to the Man,"[21] for me, one of the most moving hymns in our Church.

Having been the foolish swimmer pulled back to safety by the very man he had sought to destroy, Phelps must have had unique appreciation for the stature of the Prophet, who truly understood and believed in the Atonement of Jesus Christ.

We all have need to repent, and we all have the obligation to forgive. True friends, magnanimous friends, genuine Latter-day Saint friends will help each other do that. I am especially moved by a line from Phelps's poignant letter to the Prophet: "I want to be saved if my friends will help me."[22] For the nearly fifty years since I first read those words, I have thought perhaps they contained the sweetest insight into the true purpose of friendship that has ever been written. Friends, true friends, lead people *out* of sin, *not into* it. They help each other repent, and they forgive past mistakes in the process. Be a true friend to those who need your strength and integrity.

One of the most encouraging and compassionate parables in all of holy writ representing the need for repentance and the power of forgiveness is the story of the prodigal son, in which the anxious father, seeing his son returning, "had compassion, and ran, and fell on his neck, and kissed him."[23] God bless us to help each other to "come to ourselves,"[24] as the scriptures say the prodigal son did. God bless us to help each other come back home. "I want to be saved if my friends will help me." I am grateful for the greatest friend any of us could ever have, in time or eternity, the Lord Jesus Christ, who has made repentance possible and who is the majestic personification of forgiveness itself. I don't know whether He will want to fall on our neck and kiss us, but for such atoning compassion I know we will want to fall at His feet and kiss Him. May we change this very day if we need to. May we embrace the Atonement and repent of our sins in anticipation of such an encounter with God.

NOTES

From a talk given March 21, 2014, at the Orem Institute of Religion.

1. Romans 3:23; emphasis added.
2. John 14:6.
3. 2 Nephi 28:21.
4. A.C. Bradley, *Shakespearean Tragedy* (1967), 276.
5. William Shakespeare, *Macbeth*, act 5, scene 3, lines 40–45.
6. Shakespeare, *Macbeth*, act 5, scene 3, lines 45–46.
7. Shakespeare, *Macbeth*, act 5, scene 5, lines 23–28.
8. Spencer W. Kimball, *The Miracle of Forgiveness* (1969), x–xii.
9. Kimball, *Miracle of Forgiveness*.
10. Mosiah 27:8.
11. Mosiah 27:10.
12. Mosiah 28:4.
13. Alma 36:13–14.
14. Mosiah 27:28.
15. Gordon B. Hinckley, "And Peter Went Out and Wept Bitterly," *Ensign*, May 1979, 65–67.
16. Acts 5:15.
17. Hinckley, "And Peter Went Out," 65–67.
18. Joseph Smith, *History of the Church of Jesus Christ of Latter-day Saints*, 7 vols. (1932–1951), 2:511.
19. Smith, *History of the Church*, 4:141–42; emphasis added.
20. Smith, *History of the Church*, 4:162–64.
21. "Praise to the Man," *Hymns of The Church of Jesus Christ of Latter-day Saints* (1985), no. 27.
22. Smith, *History of the Church*, 4:141–42.
23. Luke 15:20.
24. See Luke 15:17.

The formula of

FAITH

IS TO HOLD ON,

WORK ON,

see it through,

AND LET THE DISTRESS OF EARLIER HOURS

(REAL OR IMAGINED)

fall away in the abundance of

THE FINAL REWARD.

To my friends who
have not understood God's grace

⁓

CHAPTER 3

The Laborers in the Vineyard

I wish to speak of the Savior's parable in which a house-holder "went out early in the morning to hire labourers." After employing the first group at 6:00 in the morning, he returned at 9:00 a.m., at 12:00 noon, and at 3:00 in the afternoon, hiring more workers as the urgency of the harvest increased. The scripture says he came back a final time, "about the eleventh hour" (approximately 5:00 p.m.), and hired a concluding number. Then, just an hour later, all the workers gathered to receive their day's wage. Surprisingly, all received the same wage in spite of the different hours of labor. Immediately, those hired first were angry, saying, "These last have wrought but one hour, and thou hast made them equal unto us, which have borne the burden and heat of the day."[1] When reading this parable, perhaps you, as well as those workers, have felt there was an injustice being done here. Let me speak briefly to that concern.

First of all, it is important to note that *no one* has been treated unfairly here. The first workers agreed to the full wage of the day, and they received it. Furthermore, they were, I can only imagine, very grateful to get the work. In the time of the Savior, an average man and his family could not do much more than live on what they made that day. If you didn't work or farm or fish or sell, you likely didn't eat. With more prospective workers than jobs, these first men chosen were the most fortunate in the entire labor pool that morning.

Indeed, if there is any sympathy to be generated, it should at least initially be for the men *not* chosen who also had mouths to feed and backs to clothe. Luck never seemed to be with some of them. With each visit of the steward throughout the day, they always saw someone else chosen.

But just at day's close, the householder returns a surprising fifth time with a remarkable eleventh-hour offer! These last and most discouraged of laborers, hearing only that they will be treated fairly, accept work without even knowing the wage, knowing that *anything* will be better than nothing, which is what they have had so far. Then as they gather for their payment, they are stunned to receive the same as all the others! How awestruck they must have been and how very, very grateful! Surely never had such compassion been seen in all their working days.

It is with that reading of the story that I feel the grumbling of the first laborers must be seen. As the householder in the parable tells them (and I paraphrase only slightly): "My friends, I am not being unfair to you. You agreed on the wage for the day, a good wage. You were very happy to get the work, and I am very happy with the way you served. You are paid in full. Take your pay and enjoy the blessing. As for the others, *surely I am free to do what I like with my own money.*" Then this piercing question to anyone then or now who needs to hear it: *"Why should you be jealous because I choose to be kind?"*

Brothers and sisters, there are going to be times in our lives when someone else gets an unexpected blessing or receives some special recognition. May I plead with us not to be hurt—and certainly not to feel envious—when good fortune comes to another person? We are not diminished when someone else is added upon. We are not in a race against each other to see who is the wealthiest or the most talented or the most beautiful or even the most blessed. The race we are *really* in is the race against sin, and surely envy is one of the most universal of those.

Furthermore, envy is a mistake that just keeps on giving. Obviously we suffer a little when some *misfortune* befalls *us,* but envy requires us to suffer all *good fortune* that befalls *everyone* we know! What a bright prospect that is—downing another quart of pickle juice every time anyone around you has a happy moment! To say nothing of the chagrin in the end, when we find that God really is both just and merciful, giving to all who stand with Him "all that he hath,"[2] as the scripture says. So lesson number one from the Lord's vineyard: coveting, pouting, or tearing others down does *not* elevate *your* standing, nor does demeaning someone else improve your self-image. So be kind, and be grateful that God is kind. It is a happy way to live.

A second point I wish to take from this parable is the sorrowful mistake some could make if they were to forgo the receipt of their wages at the *end* of the day because they were preoccupied with perceived problems *earlier* in the day. It doesn't say here that anyone threw his coin in the householder's face and stormed off penniless, but I suppose one might have.

My beloved brothers and sisters, what happened in this story at 9:00 or noon or 3:00 is swept up in the grandeur of the universally generous payment at the end of the day. The formula of faith is to hold on, work on, see it through, and let the distress of earlier hours—real or imagined—fall away in the abundance of the final reward. Don't dwell on old issues or grievances—not toward yourself nor your neighbor nor even, I might add, toward this true and living Church. The majesty of your life, of your neighbor's life, and of the gospel of Jesus Christ will be made manifest at the last day, even if such majesty is not always recognized by everyone in the early going. So don't hyperventilate about something that happened at 9:00 in the morning when the grace of God is trying to reward you at 6:00 in the evening—whatever your labor arrangements have been through the day.

We consume such precious emotional and spiritual capital

clinging tenaciously to the memory of a discordant note we struck in a childhood piano recital, or something a spouse said or did twenty years ago that we are determined to hold over his or her head for another twenty, or an incident in Church history that proved no more or less than that mortals will always struggle to measure up to the immortal hopes placed before them. Even if one of those grievances did not originate with you, it can end with you. And what a reward there will be for that contribution when the Lord of the vineyard looks you in the eye and accounts are settled at the end of our earthly day.

Which leads me to my third and last point. This parable—like all parables—is not really about laborers or wages any more than the others are about sheep and goats. This is a story about God's goodness, His patience and forgiveness, and the Atonement of the Lord Jesus Christ. It is a story about generosity and compassion. It is a story about grace. It underscores the thought I heard many years ago that surely the thing God enjoys most about being God is the thrill of being merciful, especially to those who don't expect it and often feel they don't deserve it.

However late you think you are, however many chances you think you have missed, however many mistakes you feel you have made or talents you think you don't have, or however far from home and family and God you feel you have traveled, I testify that you have *not* traveled beyond the reach of divine love. It is not possible for you to sink lower than the infinite light of Christ's Atonement shines.

Whether you are not yet of our faith or were with us once and have not remained, there is nothing in either case that you have done that cannot be undone. There is no problem you cannot overcome. There is no dream that in the unfolding of time and eternity cannot yet be realized. Even if you feel you are the lost and last laborer of the eleventh hour, the Lord of the vineyard still stands beckoning. "Come boldly [to] the throne of grace,"[3] and fall at the feet of the Holy One of Israel. Come and feast "without money and without price"[4] at the table of the Lord.

I especially make an appeal for husbands and fathers, priesthood bearers or prospective priesthood bearers, to, as Lehi said, "Awake! and arise from the dust . . . and be men."[5] Not always but often it is the men who choose not to answer the call to "come join the ranks."[6] Women and children frequently seem more willing. Brethren, step up. Do it for your sake. Do it for the sake of those who love you and are praying that you will respond. Do it for the sake of the Lord Jesus Christ, who paid an unfathomable price for the future He wants you to have.

To those of you who have been blessed by the gospel for many years because you were fortunate enough to find it early, to those of you who have come to the gospel by stages and phases later, and to those of you—members and not yet members—who may still be hanging back, to each of you, one and all, I testify of the renewing power of God's love and the miracle of His grace. *His concern is for the faith at which you finally arrive, not the hour of the day in which you got there.*

So if you have made covenants, keep them. If you haven't made them, make them. If you have made them and broken them, repent and repair them. It is *never* too late so long as the Master of the vineyard says there is time. Please listen to the prompting of the Holy Spirit telling you right now, this very moment, that you should accept the atoning gift of the Lord Jesus Christ and enjoy the fellowship of His labor. Don't delay. It's getting late.

NOTES

From a talk given at general conference, April 2012.

1. See Matthew 20:1–15.
2. Luke 12:44.
3. Hebrews 4:16.
4. Isaiah 55:1.
5. 2 Nephi 1:14, 21.
6. "We Are All Enlisted," *Hymns of The Church of Jesus Christ of Latter-day Saints* (1985), no. 250.

THE PATH OF

salvation

always goes through

GETHSEMANE

To my friends
who face opposition

⟿⟿

CHAPTER 4

LESSONS FROM LIBERTY JAIL

One of the great blessings of our assignments as General Authorities is the chance to visit members of the Church in various locations around the world and to glean from the history that our members have experienced across the globe. In that spirit I wish to share some feelings that came to me during a Church assignment I had to visit the Platte City stake in western Missouri.

The Platte City Missouri Stake lies adjacent to the Liberty Missouri Stake, now a famous location in Church history encompassing several important Church history sites, including the Liberty Jail. From your study of Church history, you will likely know something of the experience the Prophet Joseph

Smith and his brethren had while imprisoned in that facility during the winter of 1838–39. This was a terribly difficult time in our history for the Church generally and certainly for the Prophet Joseph himself, who bore the brunt of the persecution in that period. Indeed, I daresay that until his martyrdom five and a half years later, there was no more burdensome time in Joseph's life than this cruel, illegal, and unjustified incarceration in Liberty Jail.

Time does not permit a detailed discussion of the experiences that led up to this moment in Church history, but suffice it to say that problems of various kinds had been building ever since the Prophet Joseph had received a revelation in July of 1831 designating Missouri as the place "consecrated for the gathering of the saints" and the building up of "the city of Zion."[1] By October of 1838, all-out war seemed inevitable between Mormon and non-Mormon forces confronting each other over these issues. After being driven from several of the counties in the western part of that state, and under the presumption they had been invited to discuss ways of defusing the volatile situation that had developed, five leaders of the Church, including the Prophet Joseph, marched under a flag of truce to the camp of the Missouri militia near the small settlement of Far West, located in Caldwell County.

As it turned out, the flag of truce was meaningless, and the Church leaders were immediately put in chains and placed under heavy guard. The morning after this arrest, two more Latter-day Saint leaders, including the Prophet's brother

Hyrum, were taken prisoner, making a total of seven in captivity.

Injustice swiftly moved forward toward potential tragedy when a military "court" convened by officers of that militia ordered that Joseph Smith and the six other prisoners all be taken to the public square at Far West and summarily shot. To his eternal credit, Brigadier General Alexander Doniphan, an officer in the Missouri forces, boldly and courageously refused to carry out the inhumane, unjustifiable order. In a daring stand that could have brought him his own court-martial, he cried out against the commanding officer: "It is cold-blooded murder. I will not obey your order. . . . And if you execute these men, I will hold you responsible before an earthly tribunal, so help me God."[2] In showing such courage and integrity, Doniphan not only saved the lives of these seven men but endeared himself to Latter-day Saints in every generation.

Their execution averted, the Church leaders were marched on foot from Far West to Independence, then from Independence to Richmond. Parley P. Pratt was remanded to nearby Daviess County for trial there, and the other six prisoners, including Joseph and Hyrum, were sent to Liberty, the county seat of neighboring Clay County, to await trial there the next spring. They arrived in Liberty on December 1, 1838, just as winter was coming on.

The jail, one of the few and certainly one of the more forbidding of such structures in that region, was considered escape proof, and it probably was. It had two stories. The top or main floor was accessible to the outside world only by a single small, heavy door. In the middle of that floor was a trapdoor through which prisoners were lowered into the lower floor or dungeon. The outside walls of the prison were of rough-hewn limestone two feet thick, with inside walls of twelve-inch oak logs. These two walls were separated by a twelve-inch space filled with loose rock. Combined, these walls made a formidable, virtually impenetrable barrier four feet thick.

In the dungeon the floor-to-ceiling height was barely six feet, and inasmuch as some of the men, including the Prophet Joseph, were over six feet tall, this meant that when standing they were constantly in a stooped position. When they lay down it was mostly upon the rough, bare stones of the prison floor, covered here and there by a bit of loose straw or an occasional dirty straw mat.

The food given to the prisoners was coarse and sometimes contaminated, so filthy that one of them said they "could not eat it until [they] were driven to it by hunger."[3] On as many as four occasions they had poison administered to them in their food, making them so violently ill that for days they alternated between vomiting and a kind of delirium, not really caring whether they lived or died. In the Prophet Joseph's letters, he spoke of the jail being a "hell, surrounded with demons . . . where we are compelled to hear nothing but blasphemous oaths, and witness a scene of blasphemy, and drunkenness and hypocrisy, and debaucheries of every description."[4] "We have . . . not blankets sufficient to keep us warm," he said, "and when we have a fire, we are obliged to have almost a constant smoke."[5] "Our souls have been bowed down"[6] and "my nerve trembles from long confinement."[7] "Pen, or tongue, or angels," Joseph wrote, could not adequately describe "the malice of hell" that he suffered there.[8] And all of this occurred during what, by some accounts, was considered then the coldest winter on record in the state of Missouri.

But it is not my purpose to dwell upon the sorrow and difficulty these men confronted in Liberty Jail. I promise I have something else in mind to say.

Most of us, most of the time, speak of the facility at Liberty as a "jail" or a "prison," and certainly it was that. But Elder Brigham H. Roberts, in recording the history of the Church, spoke of the facility as a temple, or, more accurately, a "prison-temple."[9] Elder Neal A. Maxwell used the same phrasing in some of his writings.[10] Certainly it lacked the purity, the beauty, the comfort, and the cleanliness of our true temples, our dedicated temples. The speech and behavior of the guards and criminals who came there was anything but templelike. In fact, the restricting brutality and injustice of this experience at Liberty would make it seem the very antithesis of the liberating, merciful spirit of our temples and the ordinances that are performed in them. So in what sense could Liberty Jail be called a "temple"—or at least a kind of temple—in the development of Joseph Smith personally and in his role as a prophet? And what does such a title tell us about God's love and teachings, including where and when that love and those teachings are made manifest?

As we think on these things, does it strike us that spiritual experience, revelatory experience, sacred experience can come to every one of us in all the many and varied stages and circumstances of our lives if we want it, if we hold on and pray on, and if we keep our faith strong through our difficulties? We love and cherish our dedicated temples and the essential, exalting ordinances that are performed there. We thank heaven and the presiding Brethren that more and more of them are being built, giving more and more of us greater access to them. They are truly the holiest, most sacred structures in the kingdom of God, to which we all ought to go as worthily and as often as possible.

But when you have to, you can have sacred, revelatory, profoundly instructive experience with the Lord in *any* situation you are in. Indeed, let me put that even a little more strongly: You can have sacred, revelatory, profoundly instructive experience with the Lord *in the most miserable experiences of your life*—in the worst settings, while enduring the most painful injustices, when facing the most insurmountable odds and opposition you have ever faced.

Now let's talk about those propositions for a moment. Every one of us, in one way or another, great or small, dramatic or incidental, is going to spend a little time in Liberty Jail—spiritually speaking. We will face things we do not want to face for reasons that may not have been our fault. Indeed, we may face difficult circumstances for reasons that were absolutely right and proper, reasons that came because we were trying to keep the commandments of the Lord. We may face persecution; we may endure heartache and separation from loved ones; we may be hungry and cold and forlorn. Yes, before our lives are over we may all be given a little taste of what the prophets faced often in their lives.

But the lessons of the winter of 1838–39 teach us that every experience can become a *redemptive* experience if we remain bonded to our Father in Heaven through that difficulty. These difficult lessons teach us that man's extremity is God's opportunity, and if we will be humble and faithful, if we will be believing and not curse God for our problems, He can turn the unfair and inhumane and debilitating prisons of our lives into temples—or at least into a circumstance that can bring comfort and revelation, divine companionship and peace.

Let me push this just a little further. I've just said that hard times *can* happen to us. President Joseph Fielding Smith, grandnephew of the Prophet Joseph and grandson of the incarcerated Hyrum, said something even stronger than that when he dedicated the Liberty Jail Visitors' Center in 1963. Alluding to the kind of history we've reviewed here and looking on the scene where his grandfather and granduncle were so unjustly held, he said perhaps such things *have* to happen—not only can they happen, perhaps they have to. Said he: "As I have read the history of those days, the days that went before and days that came after, I have reached the conclusion that the hardships, the persecution, the almost universal opposition [toward the Church at that time] were *necessary*. At any rate they became school teachers to our people. They helped to make [them] strong."[11]

Without trying to determine which of these kinds of experiences in our life are "mandatory" and which are "optional" but still good for us, may I suggest just a very few of the lessons learned at Liberty—those experiences that were "school teachers" to Joseph and can be to us, experiences that contribute so much to our education in mortality and our exaltation in eternity.

In selecting these lessons I note yet another kind of blessing that came out of this adversity. To make the points that I am now going to try to make, I have drawn directly upon the revelatory words that came from the lips of Joseph Smith during this heartbreaking time, words that we now have canonized as sacred scripture in the Doctrine and Covenants. I guess we're not supposed to have favorite scriptures, and I have enough of them that you won't be able to pin me down to one or two, but certainly any list of my favorite scriptures would have to include those written from the darkness of Liberty Jail.

What we instantly learn is that God was not only teaching Joseph Smith in that prison circumstance but He was teaching *all* of us, for generations yet to come. What a scriptural gift! And what a high price was paid for it! But how empty would our lives as Latter-day Saints be if we did not have sections 121, 122, and 123 of the Doctrine and Covenants. They are contained in total on a mere seven pages of text, but those seven pages will touch your heart with their beauty and their power. And they will remind you that God often "moves in a mysterious way His wonders to perform."[12] In any case, He certainly turned adversity into blessing in giving us those sacred writings and reflections, so pure, noble, and Christian in both tone and content, yet produced in such an impure, ignoble, and unchristian setting.

The first lesson of Liberty Jail is inherent in what I've already said—that everyone, including (and perhaps especially) the righteous, will be called upon to face trying times. When that happens we can sometimes fear God has abandoned us, and we might be left, at least for a time, to wonder when our troubles will ever end. As individuals, as families, as communities, and as nations, probably everyone has had or will have occasion to feel as Joseph Smith felt when he asked why such sorrow had to come and how long its darkness and damage would remain. We identify with him when he cries from the depth and discouragement of his confinement: "O God, where art thou? . . . How long shall thy hand be stayed . . . ? Yea, O Lord, how long shall [thy people] suffer . . . before . . . thy bowels be moved with compassion toward them?"[13]

That is a painful, personal cry—a cry from the heart, a spiritual loneliness we may all have occasion to feel at some time in our lives.

Whenever these moments of our extremity come, we must not succumb to the fear that God has abandoned us or that He does not hear our prayers. He *does* hear us. He *does* see us. He *does* love us. When we are in dire circumstances and want to cry "Where art Thou?" it is imperative that we remember He is right there with us—where He has always been! We must continue to believe, continue to have faith, continue to pray and plead with heaven, even if we feel for a time that our prayers are not heard and that God has somehow gone away. He *is* there. Our prayers *are* heard. And when we weep, He and the angels of heaven weep with us.

When lonely, cold, hard times come, we have to endure, we have to continue, we have to persist. That was the Savior's message in the parable of the importuning widow.[14] Keep knocking on that door. Keep pleading. In the meantime, know that God hears your cries and knows your distress. He is your Father, and you are His child.

When what has to be has been and when the lessons to be learned have been learned, it will be for us as it was for the Prophet Joseph. The time he felt most alone and distant from heaven's ear was the very time he received the wonderful ministration of the Spirit and the glorious answers that came from his Father in Heaven. Into this dismal dungeon and this depressing time, the voice of God came, saying:

"My son, peace be unto thy soul; thine adversity and thine afflictions shall be but a small moment;

"And then, if thou endure it well, God shall exalt thee on high; thou shalt triumph over all thy foes."[15]

Even though seemingly unjust circumstances may be heaped

upon us and unkind and unmerited things may be done to us—perhaps by those we consider enemies but also, in some cases, by those who we thought were friends—nevertheless, through it all, *God is with us.* I am reminded of the traditional Christian hymn "Nearer, My God, to Thee" with its seldom-sung fourth verse:

> *Out of my stony griefs*
> *Bethel I'll raise;*
> *So by my woes to be*
> *Nearer, my God, to thee.*[16]

We are not alone in our little prisons here. When suffering, we may in fact be nearer to God than we've ever been in our entire lives. That knowledge can turn every such situation into a would-be temple.

Regarding our earthly journey, the Lord has promised: "I will go before your face. I will be on your right hand and on your left, and my Spirit shall be in your hearts, and mine angels round about you, to bear you up."[17] That is an everlasting declaration of God's love and care for us, including—and perhaps especially—in times of trouble.

The second lesson of Liberty Jail is that even the worthy will suffer. We need to realize that just because difficult things happen—sometimes unfair and seemingly unjustified things—it does not mean that we are unrighteous or that we are unworthy of blessings or that God is disappointed in us. Of course sinfulness does bring suffering, and the only answer to that behavior is repentance. But sometimes suffering comes to the righteous, too.

You will recall that from the depths of Liberty Jail, when Joseph was reminded that he had indeed been "cast . . . into trouble," had passed through tribulation and been falsely accused, had been torn away from his family and cast into a pit, into the hands of murderers, nevertheless, he was to remember that *the same thing had happened to the Savior of the world,* and because He was triumphant, so shall we be.[18] In giving us this sober reminder of what the Savior went through, the revelation from Liberty Jail records: "The Son of Man hath descended below them all. Art thou greater than he?"[19]

No. Joseph was not greater than the Savior, and neither are we. When we promise to follow Jesus Christ, to walk in His footsteps and be His disciples, we are promising to go where that divine path leads us. And the path of salvation always goes through Gethsemane. If the Savior faced such injustices and discouragements, such persecutions, unrighteousness, and suffering, that certainly underscores the fact that the righteous—in His case, the personification of righteousness—can be totally worthy before God and still suffer.

In fact, it ought to be a matter of great doctrinal consolation to us that Jesus, in the course of the Atonement, experienced all of the heartache and sorrow, all of the disappointments and injustices that the entire family of man had experienced and would experience—from Adam and Eve to the end of the world—in order that we would not have to face them so severely or so deeply. However heavy our load might be, it would be a lot heavier if the Savior had not gone that way before us and carried that burden with us and for us.

Very early in the Prophet Joseph's ministry, the Savior taught him this doctrine. After speaking of sufferings so exquisite to feel and so hard to bear, Jesus said, "I, God, have suffered these things for all, that they [and that means you and me and everyone] might not suffer if they would repent."[20] In our moments of pain and trial, we would shudder to think it could be worse, but the truth is clearly that it *could* be worse and it *would* be worse. Only through our faith and repentance and obedience to the gospel that provided the sacred Atonement is it kept from *being* worse.

Furthermore, we note that not only has the Savior suffered, in His case entirely innocently, but so have most of the prophets and other great men and women whose stories are recorded in the scriptures. Name an Old Testament or Book of Mormon prophet, name a New Testament Apostle, name virtually any of the leaders in any dispensation, including our own, and you name someone who has had trouble.

My point? If you are having a bad day, you've got a lot of company—very, very good company. The best company that has ever lived.

Now, don't misunderstand. We don't have to look for sorrow. We don't have to seek to be martyrs. Trouble has a way of finding us even without our looking for it. But when it is obvious that a little time in Liberty Jail waits before you (spiritually speaking), remember these first two truths taught to Joseph in that prison-temple: First, God has *not* forgotten you, and second, the Savior has been where you have been, allowing Him to provide for your deliverance and your comfort.

As the prophet Isaiah wrote, the Lord has "graven thee upon the palms of [His] hands," permanently written right there in scar tissue with Roman nails as the writing instrument. Having paid that price in the suffering that They have paid for you, the Father and the Son will never forget nor forsake you in your suffering.[21] They have planned, prepared, and guaranteed your victory if you desire it, so be believing and "endure it well."[22] In the end it "shall be for thy good,"[23] and you will see "everlasting dominion" flow unto you forever and ever "without compulsory means."[24]

Thirdly, may I remind us all that in the midst of these difficult feelings when one could justifiably be angry or reactionary or vengeful, wanting to return an eye for an eye and a tooth for a tooth, the Lord reminds us from the Liberty Jail prison-temple that "the rights of the priesthood are inseparably connected with the powers of heaven, and that the powers of heaven cannot be controlled nor handled only [or 'except'] upon the principles of righteousness."[25] Therefore, even when we face such distressing circumstances in our lives and there is something in us that wants to strike out at God or man or friend or foe, we must remember that "no power or influence *can* or *ought* to be maintained [except] . . . by persuasion, by long-suffering, by gentleness and meekness, and by love un-feigned; . . . without hypocrisy, and without guile."[26]

It has always been a wonderful testimony to me of the Prophet Joseph's greatness and the greatness of all of our prophets, including and especially the Savior of the world in His magnificence, that in the midst of such distress and diffi-culty they could remain calm and patient, charitable and for-giving—that they could even talk that way, let alone live that way. But they could, and they did. They remembered their covenants, they disciplined themselves, and they knew that we must live the gospel at all times, not just when it is convenient and not just when things are going well. Indeed, they knew that the real test of our faith and our Christian discipleship is when things are *not* going smoothly. That is when we get to see what we're made of and how strong our commitment to the gospel really is.

Surely the classic example of this is that in the most painful hours of the Crucifixion the Savior could say, "Father, forgive them; for they know not what they do."[27] That is a hard thing to ask when we're hurting. That is a hard thing to do when we've been offended or are tired or stressed out or suffering in-nocently. But that is when Christian behavior may matter the most. Remember, "the powers of heaven cannot be controlled nor handled [except] upon the principles of righteousness." And do we need the powers of heaven with us at such times! As Joseph was taught in this prison-temple, even in distress and sorrow we must "let [our] bowels . . . be full of charity towards all men . . . ; then [and only then] shall [our] confidence wax strong in the presence of God; and . . . the Holy Ghost shall be [our] constant companion."[28]

Remaining true to our Christian principles is the only way we can have divine influence to help us. The Spirit has a near-impossible task to get through to a heart that is filled with hate or anger or vengeance or self-pity. Those are all antithetical to the Spirit of the Lord. On the other hand, the Spirit finds instant access to a heart striving to be charitable and forgiving, long-suffering and kind—principles of true discipleship. What a testimony that gospel principles are to apply at all times and in all situations, and that if we strive to remain faithful, the triumph of a Christian life can never be vanquished, no matter how grim the circumstance might be! How I love the majesty of these elegant, celestial teachings taught, ironically, in such a despicable setting and time.

As a valedictory to the lessons from Liberty Jail, I refer to the final canonized statement of that prison-temple experience, in which the Lord says to us through His prophet, Joseph Smith, "Therefore, dearly beloved brethren [and sisters, when we are in even the most troubling of times], let us *cheerfully* do all things that lie in our power; and then may we stand still, with the utmost assurance, to see the salvation of God, and for his arm to be revealed."[29]

What a tremendously optimistic and faithful concluding declaration to be issued from a prison-temple! When he wrote those lines, Joseph did not know when he would be released or if he would ever be released. There was every indication that his enemies were still planning to take his life.

Furthermore, his wife and children were alone, frightened, often hungry, wondering how they would fend for themselves without their husband and father. The Saints, too, were without homes and without their prophet. They were leaving Missouri, heading for Illinois, but who knew what tragedies were awaiting them there? Surely it was the bleakest and darkest of times.

Yet in these cold, lonely hours, Joseph says, let us do all we can and *do it cheerfully*. And then we can justifiably turn to the Lord, wait upon His mercy, and see His arm revealed in our behalf.

What a magnificent attitude to maintain in good times or bad, in sorrow or in joy!

I testify that the Father and the Son do live. And I testify that They are close, perhaps even closest via the Holy Spirit, when we are experiencing difficult times. I testify that heaven's kindness will never depart from you, regardless of what happens.[30] I testify that bad days come to an end, that faith always triumphs, and that heavenly promises are always kept. I testify that God is our Father, that Jesus is the Christ, that this is the true and living gospel—found in this, the true and living Church. In the words of the Liberty Jail prison-temple experience, my friends, "Hold on thy way. . . . Fear not . . . , for God shall be with you forever and ever."[31]

NOTES

From a talk given September 7, 2008, at a Church Educational System fireside.

1. Doctrine and Covenants 57:1, 2.
2. In Joseph Smith, *History of the Church of Jesus Christ of Latter-day Saints,* 7 vols. (1932–1951), 3:190–91.
3. Alexander McRae, in B. H. Roberts, *A Comprehensive History of the Church,* 6 vols. (1930), 1:521.
4. Smith, *History of the Church,* 3:290.
5. Letter to Isaac Galland, March 22, 1839, in *Personal Writings of Joseph Smith,* rev. ed., comp. Dean C. Jessee (2002), 456.
6. Letter to the Church in Caldwell County, December 16, 1838; "Communications," *Times and Seasons,* April 1840, 85.
7. Letter to Emma Smith, March 21, 1839, in *Personal Writings,* 449.
8. Letter to Emma Smith, April 4, 1839, in *Personal Writings,* 463, 464; spelling and capitalization standardized.
9. See Roberts, *Comprehensive History,* 1:521, chapter heading; see also 526.
10. See, for example, Neal A. Maxwell, "A Choice Seer," *Ensign,* August 1986, 12.
11. "Text of Address by Pres. Smith at Liberty Jail Rites," *Church News,* September 21, 1963, 14; emphasis added.
12. "God Moves in a Mysterious Way," *Hymns of The Church of Jesus Christ of Latter-day Saints* (1985), no. 285.
13. Doctrine and Covenants 121:1–3.
14. See Luke 18:1–8; see also Luke 11:5–10.
15. Doctrine and Covenants 121:7–8.
16. "Nearer, My God, to Thee," *Hymns,* no. 100; emphasis added.
17. Doctrine and Covenants 84:88.
18. See Doctrine and Covenants 122:4–8.
19. Doctrine and Covenants 122:8.
20. Doctrine and Covenants 19:16.
21. See Isaiah 49:14–16; 1 Nephi 21:14–16.
22. Doctrine and Covenants 121:8.
23. Doctrine and Covenants 122:7.
24. Doctrine and Covenants 121:46.

25. Doctrine and Covenants 121:36.
26. Doctrine and Covenants 121:41–42; emphasis added.
27. Luke 23:34.
28. Doctrine and Covenants 121:45–46.
29. Doctrine and Covenants 123:17; emphasis added.
30. See Isaiah 54:7–10; 3 Nephi 22:7–10.
31. Doctrine and Covenants 122:9.

I n this Church,

what we *know*

will always

trump what we

do not know.

And remember,

in this world,

everyone is to

WALK BY FAITH.

To my friends
who long to believe

CHAPTER 5

"LORD, I BELIEVE"

On one occasion Jesus came upon a group arguing vehemently with His disciples. When the Savior inquired as to the cause of this contention, the father of an afflicted child stepped forward, saying he had approached Jesus's disciples for a blessing for his son, but they were not able to provide it. With the boy still gnashing his teeth, foaming from the mouth, and thrashing on the ground in front of them, the father appealed to Jesus with what must have been last-resort desperation in his voice:

"If thou canst do any thing," he said, "have compassion on us, and help us.

"Jesus said unto him, If thou canst believe, all things are possible to him that believeth.

"And straightway the father of the child cried out, and said with tears, Lord, I believe; help thou mine unbelief."[1]

This man's initial conviction, by his own admission, is limited. But he has an urgent, emphatic desire in behalf of his child. We are told that is good enough for a beginning. "Even if ye can no more than *desire to believe*," Alma declares, "let this desire work in you, even until ye believe."[2] With no other hope remaining, this father asserts what faith he has and pleads with the Savior of the world, "If *thou* canst do *any thing*, have compassion on *us*, and help *us*."[3] I can hardly read those words without weeping. The plural pronoun *us* is obviously used intentionally. This man is saying, in effect, "Our whole family is pleading. Our struggle never ceases. We are exhausted. Our son falls into the water. He falls into the fire. He is continually in danger, and we are continually afraid. We don't know where else to turn. Can *you* help us? We will be grateful for *anything*—a partial blessing, a glimmer of hope, some small lifting of the burden carried by this boy's mother every day of her life."

"If *thou* canst do *any thing*," spoken by the father, comes back to him "If *thou* canst *believe*," spoken by the Master.[4]

"Straightway," the scripture says—not slowly nor skeptically nor cynically but "straightway"—the father cries out in his unvarnished parental pain, "Lord, I believe; help thou mine unbelief." In response to new and still partial faith, Jesus heals the boy, almost literally raising him from the dead, as Mark describes the incident.[5]

With this tender scriptural record as a backdrop, I wish to address these thoughts directly to the young people of the Church—young in years of age or young in years of membership or young in years of faith. One way or another, that should include just about all of us.

Observation number one regarding this account is that when facing the challenge of faith, the father asserts his strength first and only then acknowledges his limitation. His initial declaration is affirmative and without hesitation: "Lord, I believe." I would say to all who wish for more faith, remember this man! In moments of fear or doubt or troubling times, hold the ground you have already won, even if that ground is limited. In the growth we all have to experience in mortality, the spiritual equivalent of this boy's affliction or this parent's desperation is going to come to all of us. When those moments come and issues surface, the resolution of which is not immediately forthcoming, *hold fast to what you already know and stand strong until additional knowledge comes.* It was of this very incident, this specific miracle, that Jesus said, "If ye have faith as a grain of mustard seed, ye shall say unto this mountain, Remove hence to yonder place; and it shall remove; and nothing shall be impossible unto you."[6] The size of your faith or the degree of your knowledge is not the issue—it is the integrity you demonstrate toward the faith you do have and the truth you already know.

The second observation is a variation of the first. When problems come and questions arise, do not start your quest for faith by saying how much you do *not* have, leading as it were with your "unbelief." That is like trying to stuff a turkey through the beak! Let me be clear on this point: I am not asking you to pretend to faith you do not have. I *am* asking you to be true to the faith you *do* have. Sometimes we act as if an honest declaration of doubt is a higher manifestation of moral courage than is an honest declaration of faith. It is not! So let us all remember the clear message of this scriptural account: Be as candid about your questions as you need to be; life is full of them on one subject or another. But if you and your family want to be healed, don't let those questions stand in the way of faith working its miracle.

Furthermore, you have more faith than you think you do because of what the Book of Mormon calls "the greatness of the evidences."[7] "Ye shall know them by their fruits," Jesus said,[8] and the fruit of living the gospel is evident in the lives of Latter-day Saints everywhere. As Peter and John said once to an ancient audience, I say today, "We cannot but speak the things which we have seen and heard," and what we have seen and heard is that "a notable miracle hath been done" in the lives of millions of members of this Church. That cannot be denied.[9]

This is a divine work in process, with the manifestations and blessings of it abounding in every direction, so please don't hyperventilate if from time to time issues arise that need to be examined, understood, and resolved. They do and they will.

In this Church, what we know will always trump what we do not know. And remember, in this world, everyone is to walk by faith.

So be kind regarding human frailty—your own as well as that of those who serve with you in a Church led by volunteer, mortal men and women. Except in the case of His only perfect Begotten Son, imperfect people are all God has ever had to work with. That must be terribly frustrating to Him, but He deals with it. So should we. And when you see imperfection, remember that the limitation is *not* in the divinity of the work. As one gifted writer has suggested, when the infinite fulness is poured forth, it is not the oil's fault if there is some loss because finite vessels can't quite contain it all.[10] Those finite vessels include you and me, so be patient and kind and forgiving.

Last observation: When doubt or difficulty comes, do not be afraid to ask for help. If we want it as humbly and honestly as this father did, we can get it. The scriptures phrase such earnest desire as being of "real intent," pursued "with full purpose of heart, acting no hypocrisy and no deception before God."[11] I testify that in response to *that* kind of importuning, God will send help from both sides of the veil to strengthen our belief.

A fourteen-year-old boy recently said to me a little hesitantly, "Brother Holland, I can't say yet that I know the Church is true, but I believe it is." I hugged that boy until his eyes bulged out. I told him with all the fervor of my soul that *belief* is a precious word, an even more precious act, and he need never apologize for "only believing." I told him that Christ Himself said, "Be not afraid, only believe,"[12] a phrase which, by the way, carried young Gordon B. Hinckley into the mission field.[13] I told this boy that belief was always the first step toward conviction and that the definitive articles of our collective faith forcefully reiterate the phrase "We believe."[14] And I told him how very proud I was of him for the honesty of his quest.

Now, with the advantage that six decades give me since I was a newly believing fourteen-year-old, I declare some things I now know. I know that God is at all times and in all ways and in all circumstances our loving, forgiving Father in Heaven. I know Jesus was His only perfect child, whose life was given lovingly by the will of both the Father and the Son for the redemption of all the rest of us who are not perfect. I know He rose from that death to live again, and because He did, you and I will also. I know that Joseph Smith, who acknowledged that he wasn't perfect,[15] was nevertheless the chosen instrument in God's hand to restore the everlasting gospel to the earth. I also know that in doing so—particularly through translating the Book of Mormon—he has taught me more of God's love, of Christ's divinity, and of priesthood power than any other prophet of whom I have ever read, known, or heard in a lifetime of seeking.

These things I declare to you with the conviction Peter called the "more sure word of prophecy."[16] What was once a tiny seed of belief for me has grown into the tree of life, so if your faith is a little tested in this or any season, I invite you to lean on mine. I know this work is God's very truth, and I know that only at our peril would we allow doubt or devils to sway us from its path. Hope on. Journey on. Honestly acknowledge your questions and your concerns, but first and forever fan the flame of your faith, because all things are possible to them that believe.

NOTES

From a talk given at general conference, April 2013.

1. Mark 9:22–24; see also verses 14–21.
2. Alma 32:27; emphasis added.
3. Mark 9:22; emphasis added.
4. Mark 9:22, 23; emphasis added.
5. See Mark 9:24–27.
6. Matthew 17:20.
7. Helaman 5:50.
8. Matthew 7:16.
9. See Acts 4:16, 20.
10. Adapted from Alfred Edersheim, *The Life and Times of Jesus the Messiah,* 2 vols. (1883), 2:108.
11. 2 Nephi 31:13.
12. Mark 5:36.
13. See Gordon B. Hinckley, in Conference Report, October 1969, 114.
14. See Articles of Faith 1:1–13.
15. See *Teachings of Presidents of the Church: Joseph Smith* (2007), 522.
16. 2 Peter 1:19.

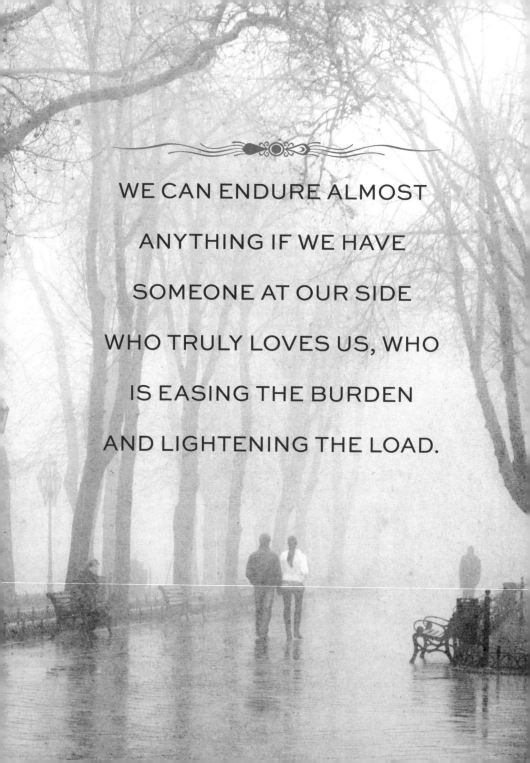

WE CAN ENDURE ALMOST
ANYTHING IF WE HAVE
SOMEONE AT OUR SIDE
WHO TRULY LOVES US, WHO
IS EASING THE BURDEN
AND LIGHTENING THE LOAD.

To my friends
who seek and share love

———

CHAPTER 6

"How Do I Love Thee?"

I wish to speak about Christlike love and what I think it can and should mean in your friendships, in your dating, in serious courtship, and ultimately in your marriage. I approach the subject knowing full well that, as a newly engaged young woman said to me last month, "There is certainly a lot of advice out there!" I don't want to add needlessly to this rhetoric on romance, but I believe that second only to your membership in the Church, your "membership in a marriage" is the most important association you will have in time and eternity—and to the faithful, what doesn't come in time will come in eternity. So perhaps you will forgive me for offering—yes—more advice. But I wish it to be scriptural advice, gospel advice, that is as basic to life as it is to love, counsel that is equally applicable to men and to women. It has nothing to do with trends or tides or tricks of the trade but has everything to do with the truth.

After a long, wonderful discourse on the subject of charity, the seventh chapter of Moroni tells us that this highest of Christian virtues is more accurately labeled "the pure love of Christ."

"And it endureth forever; and whoso is found possessed of it at the last day, it shall be well with him [and her].

"Wherefore, . . . pray unto the Father with all the energy of heart, that ye may be filled with this love, which he hath bestowed upon all who are true followers of his Son, Jesus Christ; that ye may become the sons [and daughters] of God; that when he shall appear we shall be like him, for we shall see him as he is; . . . that we may be purified even as he is pure."[1]

True charity, the absolutely pure love of Christ, has really been known only once in this world—in the form of Christ Himself, the living Son of the living God. It is Christ's love that Mormon goes to some length to describe for us and of which Paul the Apostle wrote to the Corinthians in New Testament times. As in everything, Christ is the only one who got it all right, did it all perfectly, loved the way we are all to try to love. But even though we fall short, that divine standard is there for us. It is a goal toward which we are to keep reaching, keep striving—and, certainly, a goal to keep appreciating.

And may I remind you, as Mormon explicitly taught, that

this love, this ability, capacity, and reciprocation we all so want, is a gift. It is "bestowed"—that is Mormon's word. It doesn't come without effort and without patience, but like salvation itself, in the end it is a gift, given by God to the "true followers of his Son, Jesus Christ." The solutions to life's problems are always gospel solutions. Not only are answers found in Christ but so is the power, the gift, the bestowal, the miracle of giving and receiving those answers. In this matter of love, no doctrine could be more encouraging to us than that.

I have taken for a title to my remarks Mrs. Browning's wonderful line "How do I love thee?"[2] I am impressed with her choice of adverb—not *when* do I love thee nor *where* do I love thee nor *why* do I love thee nor *why don't* you love me, but rather *how. How* do I demonstrate it, *how* do I reveal my true love for you? Mrs. Browning was correct. Real love is best shown in the "how," and it is with the how that Mormon and Paul help us the most.

The first element of divine love—pure love—taught by these two prophets is its kindness, its selfless quality, its lack of ego and vanity and consuming self-centeredness. "Charity suffereth long, and is kind, [charity] envieth not, and is not puffed up, seeketh not her own."[3] I have heard prophets teach publicly and privately what I suppose all leaders have said— that most problems in love and marriage ultimately start with selfishness. In outlining the ideal love in which Christ, the most unselfish man who ever lived, is the great example, it is not surprising that this scriptural commentary starts here.

Surely among the very first and most basic of qualities we would want to cultivate in a relationship will be that of care and sensitivity toward others, a minimum of self-centeredness that allows compassion, and courtesy to be evident. "That best portion of a good man's life [is] his . . . kindness," said Mr. Wordsworth.[4] There are lots of limitations in all of us that we hope our sweethearts will overlook. I suppose no one is as handsome or beautiful as he or she wishes, or as brilliant in school, or as witty in speech, or as wealthy as we would like. But in a world of such varied talents and fortunes, which we can't always command, I think that makes even more attractive the qualities we *can* command—such qualities as thoughtfulness, patience, a kind word, true delight in the accomplishment of others. These cost us *nothing* and they can mean *everything* to the one who receives them.

I like Mormon's and Paul's language that says one who truly loves is *not* "puffed up." "Puffed up!" Isn't that a great image! Haven't you ever been with someone who was so conceited, so full of themselves that they sounded like the Pillsbury Dough Boy? Fred Allen said once that he saw such a fellow walking down Lover's Lane holding his own hand. True love blooms when we care more about another person than we care about ourselves. That is Christ's great atoning example for us, and it ought to be more evident in the kindness we show, the respect we give, the selflessness and courtesy we employ in our personal relationships.

Love is a fragile thing, and some elements in life can try

to break it. Much damage can be done if we are not in tender hands, caring hands. To give ourselves totally to another person as we do in marriage is the most trusting step we take in any human relationship. It is a real act of faith, faith all of us must be willing to exercise. If we do it right, we end up sharing everything—all our hopes, all our fears, all our dreams, all our weaknesses—with another person.

No serious courtship or engagement or marriage is worth the name if we do not fully invest *all* that we have in it and in so doing trust ourselves totally to the one we love. You cannot succeed in love if you keep one foot out on the bank for safety's sake. The very nature of the endeavor requires that you hold on to each other as tightly as you can and jump in the pool together. In that spirit, and the spirit of Mormon's plea for pure love, I want to impress upon you the vulnerability and delicacy of your partner's future as it is placed in your hands for safekeeping. Male and female, it works both ways.

Sister Holland and I have been married for more than fifty years. I may not know everything about her, but I know half a century's worth, and she knows that much of me. I know her likes and dislikes, and she knows mine. I know her tastes and interests, hopes and dreams, and she knows mine. As our love has grown and our relationship has matured, we have been increasingly free with each other about all of that.

The result is that I know much more clearly now how to help her and, if I let myself, I know exactly what will hurt her. In the honesty of our love—love that can't truly be Christlike

without such total devotion—surely God will hold me accountable for any pain I cause her by intentionally exploiting or hurting her when she has been so trusting of me, long since having
thrown away any self-protection in order that we could be, as
the scripture says, "one flesh."[5] To impair or impede her in *any
way* for my gain or vanity or emotional mastery over her should
disqualify me to be her husband. Indeed it should consign my
miserable soul to eternal incarceration in that large and spacious
building that Lehi says is the prison of those who live by "vain
imaginations and the pride of the world."[6] No wonder that
building is at the opposite end of the field from the tree of life
representing the love of God! In all that Christ was, He was not
ever envious or inflated, never consumed with His own needs.
He did not once, *not ever* seek His own advantage at the expense of someone else. He delighted in the happiness of others,
happiness He could bring them. He was forever kind.

Members of the First Presidency have taught that "any form
of physical or mental abuse to any woman is not worthy of any
priesthood holder" and that no "man who holds the priesthood
of God [should] abuse his wife in any way, [or] demean or injure
or take undue advantage of [any] woman."[7]—and that includes
friends, dates, sweethearts and fiancées, to say nothing of wives.

The second segment of this scriptural sermon on love says
that true charity, real love, is "not easily provoked, thinketh
no evil, and rejoiceth not in iniquity." Think of how many
arguments would be avoided, how many hurt feelings could be
spared, how many cold shoulders and silent treatments could

be ended, and, in a worst-case scenario, how many breakups and divorces could be avoided if we were not so easily provoked, if we thought no evil of one another, if we not only did not rejoice in iniquity but didn't rejoice even in little mistakes.

Temper tantrums aren't cute even in children; they are despicable in adults, especially adults who are supposed to love each other. We are too easily provoked. We are too inclined to think that our partners meant to hurt us, meant to do us evil, so to speak, and in defensive or jealous response we too often rejoice when we then see *them* make a mistake and find *them* in a fault. Let's show some discipline on this one. Act a little more maturely. Bite your tongue if you have to. "He that is slow to anger is better than the mighty; and he that ruleth his spirit than he that taketh a city."[8] At least one difference between a tolerable marriage and a great one may be that willingness in the latter to allow some things to pass without comment, without response.

In a talk on love and romance you might well expect a Shakespearean reference to Romeo and Juliet. But let me refer to a much less virtuous story. With Romeo and Juliet the outcome was a result of innocence gone awry, a kind of sad, heartbreaking mistake between two families that should have known better. But in the tale of Othello and Desdemona the sorrow and destruction is calculated—it is maliciously driven from the beginning. Of all the villains in Shakespeare's writing, and perhaps in all of literature, there is no one I loathe so much as I loathe Iago. Even his name sounds evil to me, or at least it has become so. And what is his evil, and Othello's tragic, near-inexcusable susceptibility to it? It is the violation of Moroni 7 and 1 Corinthians 13. Among other things, they sought for evil where none existed, they embraced imaginary iniquity, the villains here "rejoiced [not] in the truth." Of the innocent Desdemona, Iago said, "I turn her virtue into pitch; / And out of her own goodness make the net / That shall enmesh them all."[9] Sowing doubt and devilish innuendo, playing on jealousy and deceit and finally murderous rage, Iago provokes Othello into taking Desdemona's life—virtue turned into pitch, goodness twisted into a fatal net.

Now, thank heavens, we are most of us not involved in infidelity, real or imagined, or in murder. But let's learn the lessons being taught. Think the best of each other, especially of those you say you love. Assume the good and doubt the bad. Encourage in yourself what Lincoln called "the better angels of our nature."[10] Othello could have been saved even in the last moment when he kissed Desdemona and her purity was so evident. "That [kiss] dost almost persuade / Justice to break her sword!"[11] he said. Well, he would have been spared her death and then his own suicide if he had broken what he considered justice's sword right then and there rather than, figuratively speaking, using it on her. This tragically sad Elizabethan tale could have had a beautifully happy ending if just one man, who then influenced another, had "[thought] no evil," had "rejoice[d] not in iniquity," but had "rejoice[d] in the truth."

Lastly, the prophets tell us that true love "beareth all things, believeth all things, hopeth all things, endureth all things."[12]

Once again, that is ultimately a description of Christ's love—He is the great example of one who bore and believed and hoped and endured. We are invited to do the same in our relationships to the best of our ability. Bear up and be strong. Be hopeful and believing. Some things in life we have no control over. These have to be endured. Some disappointments have to be lived with in love and marriage. These are not things anyone wants in life but sometimes they come. And when they come, we have to bear them, we have to believe, we have to hope for an end to such sorrows and difficulty, we have to endure until things come right in the end.

One of the great purposes of true love is to help each other in these times. No one ought to have to face such trials alone. We can endure almost anything if we have someone at our side who truly loves us, who is easing the burden and lightening the load. In this regard a friend from the faculty of Brigham Young University, Professor Brent Barlow, told me some years ago about Plimsoll marks.

As a youth in England, Samuel Plimsoll was fascinated with watching ships load and unload their cargoes. He soon observed that regardless of the cargo space available, each ship had its maximum capacity. If a ship exceeded its limit, it would likely sink at sea. In 1868, Plimsoll entered Parliament and passed a merchant shipping act that, among other things, called for making calculations of how much a ship could carry. As a result, lines were drawn on the hull of each ship. As the cargo was loaded, the freighter would sink lower and lower into the water. When the water level on the side of the ship reached the Plimsoll mark, the ship was considered loaded to capacity regardless of how much space remained. As a result, British deaths at sea were greatly reduced.

Like ships, people have differing capacities at different times and even different days in their lives. In our relationships we need to establish our own Plimsoll marks and help identify them in the lives of those we love. Together we need to monitor the load levels and be helpful in shedding or at least readjusting some cargo if we see our sweethearts sinking. Then, when the ship of love is stabilized, we can evaluate long term what has to continue, what can be put off until another time, and what can be put off permanently. Friends, sweethearts, and spouses need to be able to monitor each other's stress and recognize the different tides and seasons of life. We owe it to each other to declare some limits and then help jettison some things if emotional health and the strength of loving relationships are at risk. Remember—pure love "beareth all things, believeth all things, hopeth all things, endureth all things" and helps loved ones do the same.

In Mormon's and Paul's final witness they declare that "charity [pure love] never faileth." It is there through thick and thin. It endures through sunshine and shadow, through darkest sorrow and on into the light. It never fails. So Christ loved us, and that is how He hoped we would love each other. In a final injunction to us He said, "A new commandment I give unto you, that ye love one another; *as I have loved you*."[13] Of course such Christlike staying power in romance and marriage requires more than any of us really have. It requires something more, an endowment from heaven. Remember Mormon's promise—that such love, the love we each yearn for and cling to, is "bestowed" upon "true followers of . . . Christ." You want capability and safety in dating and romance, in married life and eternity? Be a true disciple of Jesus; be a genuine, committed word-and-deed Latter-day Saint. Believe that your faith has *everything* to do with your romance because it does. Jesus Christ, the Light of the World, is the only lamp by which you can successfully see the path of love and happiness for you and for your sweetheart. How *should* I love thee? As He does, for that way "never faileth."

NOTES

From a talk given February 15, 2000, at a Brigham Young University devotional.

1. Moroni 7:47–48.
2. Elizabeth Barrett Browning, *Sonnets from the Portuguese* (1850), no. 43.
3. Moroni 7:45.
4. William Wordsworth, "Lines Composed a Few Miles above Tintern Abbey" (1798), lines 33–35.
5. Genesis 2:24.
6. See 1 Nephi 11:36; 12:18.
7. James E. Faust, "The Highest Place of Honor," *Ensign*, May 1988, 37; Gordon B. Hinckley, "Reach Out in Love and Kindness," *Ensign*, November 1982, 77.
8. Proverbs 16:32.
9. William Shakespeare, *Othello*, act 2, scene 3, lines 366–68.
10. Abraham Lincoln, First Inaugural Address, March 4, 1861.
11. Shakespeare, *Othello*, act 5, scene 2, lines 16–17.
12. 1 Corinthians 13:7.
13. John 13:34; emphasis added.

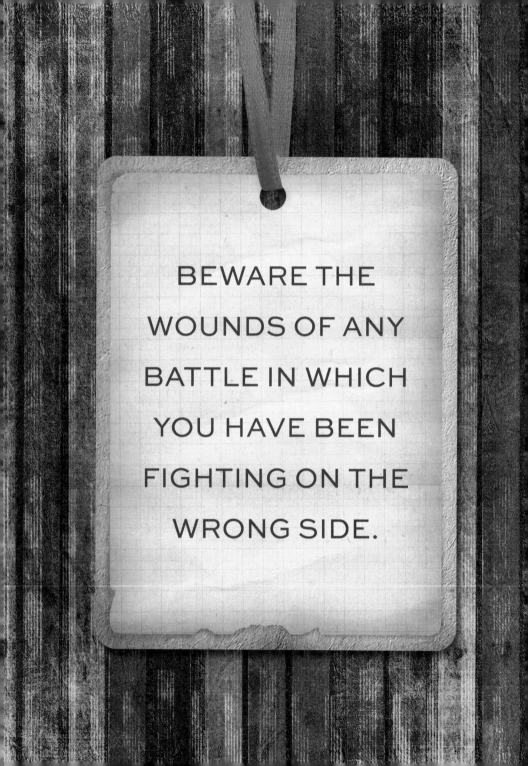

BEWARE THE WOUNDS OF ANY BATTLE IN WHICH YOU HAVE BEEN FIGHTING ON THE WRONG SIDE.

To my friends
who would be clean

⟋⟍

CHAPTER 7

PERSONAL PURITY

As modern winds of immorality swirl luridly around them, I am concerned for any of our youth or young adults who may be confused about principles of personal purity, about obligations of total chastity before marriage and complete fidelity after it. Against what is happening in the world they see and hear, and hoping to fortify parents as they teach their children a higher standard, I wish to discuss moral cleanliness. Because this subject is as sacred as any I know, I have earnestly prayed for the Holy Spirit to guide me in remarks that are more candid than I would wish to make. I know how Jacob in the Book of Mormon felt when he said on the same topic, "It grieveth me that I must use so much boldness of speech."[1]

In approaching this subject I do not document a host of social ills for which the statistics are as grim as the examples are offensive. Nor will I present here a checklist of do's and don'ts about dating and boy-girl relationships. What I wish to do is more personal—I wish to try to answer questions some of you may have been asking: *Why* should we be morally clean? *Why* is it such an important issue to God? Does the Church *have* to be so strict about it when others don't seem to be? How could anything society exploits and glamorizes so openly be very sacred or serious?

May I begin with a lesson from civilization's long, instructive story. Will and Ariel Durant have written: "No man [or woman], however brilliant or well-informed, can . . . safely . . . dismiss . . . the wisdom of [lessons learned] in the laboratory of history. A youth boiling with hormones will wonder why he should not give full freedom to his sexual desires; [but] if he is unchecked by custom, morals, or laws, he may ruin his life before he . . . understand[s] that sex is a river of fire that must be banked and cooled by a hundred restraints if it is not to consume in chaos both the individual and the group."[2]

A more important scriptural observation is offered by the writer of Proverbs: "Can a man take fire in his bosom, and his clothes not be burned? Can one go upon hot coals, and his feet not be burned? . . . Whoso committeth adultery . . . destroyeth his own soul. A wound and dishonour shall he get; and his reproach shall not be wiped away."[3]

Why is this matter of sexual relationships so severe that fire is almost always the metaphor, with passion pictured vividly in flames? What is there in the potentially hurtful heat of this that leaves one's soul—or the whole world, for that matter—destroyed if that flame is left unchecked and those passions unrestrained? What is there in all of this that prompts Alma to warn his son Corianton that sexual transgression is "an abomination in the sight of the Lord; yea, most abominable above all sins save it be the shedding of innocent blood or denying the Holy Ghost?"[4]

By assigning such seriousness to a physical appetite so universally bestowed, what is God trying to tell us about its place in His plan for all men and women? I submit to you He is doing precisely that—commenting about the very plan of life itself. Clearly among His greatest concerns regarding mortality are how one gets into this world and how one gets out of it. He has set very strict limits in these matters.

Fortunately, in the case of how life is terminated, most seem to be quite responsible. But in the significance of *giving* life, we sometimes find near-criminal irresponsibility. May I offer three reasons why this is an issue of such magnitude and consequence in the gospel of Jesus Christ.

First is the revealed, restored doctrine of the human soul.

One of the "plain and precious" truths restored in this dispensation is that "the spirit and the body are the soul of man"[5] and that when the spirit and body are separated, men and women "cannot receive a fulness of joy."[6] That is the reason why obtaining a body is so fundamentally important in the first place, why sin of any kind is such a serious matter (namely because it is sin that ultimately brings both physical and spiritual death), and why the resurrection of the body is so central to the great triumph of Christ's Atonement.

The body is an essential part of the soul. This distinctive and very important Latter-day Saint doctrine underscores why sexual sin is so serious. We declare that one who uses the God-given body of another without divine sanction abuses the very soul of that individual, abuses the central purpose and processes of life, "the very key"[7] to life, as President Boyd K. Packer once called it. In exploiting the body of another—which means exploiting his or her soul—one desecrates the Atonement of Christ, which saved that soul and which makes possible the gift of eternal life. And when one mocks the Son of Righteousness, one steps into a realm of heat hotter and holier than the noonday sun. You cannot do so and not be burned.

Please, never say: "Who does it hurt? Why not a little freedom? I can transgress now and repent later." Please don't be so foolish and so cruel. You cannot with impunity "crucify Christ afresh."[8] "Flee fornication,"[9] Paul cries, and flee *"anything like unto it,"*[10] the Doctrine and Covenants adds. Why? Well, for one reason because of the incalculable suffering in both body and spirit endured by the Savior of the world so that we *could* flee.[11] We owe Him something for that. Indeed, we owe Him everything for that. "Ye are not your own," Paul says. "Ye [have been] bought with a price: therefore *glorify God in your body, and in your spirit, which are God's.*"[12] In sexual transgression the soul is at stake—the body and the spirit.

Secondly, may I stress that human intimacy is reserved for a married couple because it is the ultimate symbol of total union, a totality and a union ordained and defined by God. From the Garden of Eden onward, marriage was intended to mean the complete merger of a man and a woman—their hearts, hopes, lives, love, family, future, everything. Adam said of Eve that she was bone of his bones and flesh of his flesh, and that they were to be "one flesh" in their life together.[13] This is a union of such completeness that we use the word *seal* to convey its eternal promise. The Prophet Joseph Smith once said we perhaps could render such a sacred bond as being "welded"[14] one to another.

But such a total union, such an unyielding commitment between a man and a woman, can only come with the proximity and permanence afforded in a marriage covenant, with solemn promises and the pledge of all they possess—their very hearts and minds, all their days and all their dreams.

Can you see the moral schism that comes from *pretending* you are one, pretending you have made solemn promises before God, sharing the physical symbols and the physical intimacy of your counterfeit union but then fleeing, retreating, severing all such other aspects of what was meant to be a total obligation?

In matters of human intimacy, you must wait! You must wait until you can give everything, and you cannot give everything until you are legally and lawfully married. To give illicitly that which is not yours to give (remember, "you are not your own") and to give only part of that which cannot be followed with the gift of your whole self is emotional Russian roulette. If you persist in pursuing physical satisfaction without the sanction of heaven, you run the terrible risk of such spiritual, psychic damage that you may undermine *both* your longing for physical intimacy *and* your ability to give wholehearted devotion to a later, truer love. You may come to that truer moment of ordained love, of real union, only to discover to your horror that what you should have saved you have spent, and that only God's grace can recover the piecemeal dissipation of the virtue you so casually gave away. On your wedding day the very best gift you can give your eternal companion is your very best self—clean and pure and worthy of such purity in return.

Thirdly, may I say that physical intimacy is not only a symbolic union between a husband and a wife—the very uniting of their souls—but it is also symbolic of a shared relationship between them and their Father in Heaven. He is immortal and perfect. We are mortal and imperfect. Nevertheless we seek ways even in mortality whereby we can unite with Him spiritually. In so doing we gain some access to both the grace and the majesty of His power. Those special moments include kneeling at a marriage altar in the house of the Lord, blessing a newborn baby, baptizing and confirming a new member of the Church, partaking of the emblems of the Lord's Supper, and so forth.

These are moments when we quite literally unite our will with God's will, our spirit with His spirit, where communion through the veil becomes very real. At such moments we not only acknowledge His divinity but we quite literally take something of that divinity to ourselves. One aspect of that divinity given to virtually all men and women is the use of His power to create a human body, that wonder of all wonders, a genetically and spiritually unique being never before seen in the history of the world and never to be duplicated again in all the ages of eternity. A child, your child—with eyes and ears and fingers and toes and a future of unspeakable grandeur.

Probably only a parent who has held that newborn infant in his or her arms understands the wonder of which I speak. Suffice it to say that of all the titles God has chosen for Himself, *Father* is the one He favors most, and *creation* is His watchword—especially human creation, creation in His image. You and I have been given something of that godliness, *but under the most serious and sacred of restrictions. The only control placed on us is self-control*—self-control born of respect for the divine sacramental power this gift represents.

My beloved friends, especially my young friends, can you see why personal purity is such a serious matter? Can you understand why the First Presidency and Council of the Twelve Apostles would issue a proclamation declaring that "the means by which mortal life is created [is] divinely appointed" and that "the sacred powers of procreation are to be employed only between man and woman, lawfully wedded as husband and wife"?[15] Don't be deceived and don't be destroyed. Unless such powers are controlled and commandments kept, your future may be burned; your world could go up in flames. Penalty may not come on the precise day of transgression, but it comes surely and certainly enough. And unless there is true repentance and obedience to a merciful God, then someday, somewhere, the morally cavalier and unclean will pray like the rich man who wished Lazarus to "dip . . . his finger in water, and cool my tongue; for I am tormented in this flame."[16]

I have declared here the solemn word of revelation that the spirit and the body constitute the soul of man, and that through the Atonement of Christ the body shall rise from the grave to unite with the spirit in an eternal existence. That body is therefore something to be kept pure and holy. Do not be afraid of soiling its hands in honest labor. Do not be afraid of scars that may come in defending the truth or fighting for the right, but beware scars that spiritually disfigure, that come to you in activities you should not have undertaken, that befall you in places where you should not have gone. Beware the wounds of any battle in which you have been fighting on the wrong side.[17]

If some few of you are carrying such wounds—and I know that you are—to you is extended the peace and renewal of repentance available through the atoning sacrifice of the Lord Jesus Christ. In such serious matters the path of repentance is not easily begun nor painlessly traveled. But the Savior of the world will walk that essential journey with you. He will strengthen you when you waver. He will be your light when it seems most dark. He will take your hand and be your hope when hope seems all you have left. His compassion and mercy, with all their cleansing and healing power, are freely given to all who truly wish complete forgiveness and will take the steps that lead to it.

I bear witness of the great plan of life, of the powers of

godliness, of mercy and forgiveness and the Atonement of the Lord Jesus Christ—all of which have profound meaning in matters of moral cleanliness. I testify that we are to glorify God in our body and in our spirit. I thank heaven for legions of the young who are doing just that and helping others do the same. I thank heaven for homes where this is taught. That lives of personal purity may be reverenced by all, I pray in the name of purity Himself, even the Lord Jesus Christ.

NOTES

From a talk given at general conference, October 1998.

1. Jacob 2:7. See Jacob 2–3 for the full context of his sermon on chastity.
2. Will and Ariel Durant, *The Lessons of History* (1968), 35–36.
3. Proverbs 6:27–28, 32–33.
4. Alma 39:5.
5. Doctrine and Covenants 88:15.
6. Doctrine and Covenants 93:34.
7. Boyd K. Packer, "Why Stay Morally Clean," *Ensign*, July 1972, 113.
8. See Hebrews 6:6.
9. 1 Corinthians 6:18.
10. Doctrine and Covenants 59:6; emphasis added.
11. See especially Doctrine and Covenants 19:15–20.
12. 1 Corinthians 6:19–20; emphasis added; see also 1 Corinthians 6:13–18.
13. See Genesis 2:23–24.
14. See Doctrine and Covenants 128:18.
15. "The Family: A Proclamation to the World," *Ensign*, November 2010, 129.
16. Luke 16:24.
17. See James E. Talmage, in Conference Report, October 1913, 117.

I AM LOOKING FOR SAINTS

young and old

WHO CARE ENOUGH ABOUT

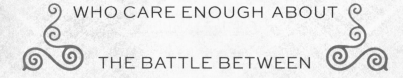

THE BATTLE BETWEEN

GOOD AND EVIL

to sign on and

SPEAK UP.

To my friends
in the army of the Lord

CHAPTER 8

"WE ARE ALL ENLISTED"

When we rehearse the grandeur of Joseph Smith's First Vision, we sometimes gloss over the menacing confrontation that came just prior to it, a confrontation intended to destroy the boy if possible but in any case to block the revelation that was to come. We don't talk about the adversary any more than we have to, and I don't like talking about him at all, but the experience of young Joseph reminds us of what every one of us needs to remember.

Number one, Satan, or Lucifer, or the father of lies—call him what you will—is real, the very personification of evil. His motives are in every case malicious, and he convulses at the appearance of redeeming light, at the very thought of truth.

Number two, he is eternally opposed to the love of God, the Atonement of Jesus Christ, and the work of peace and salvation. He will fight against these whenever and wherever he can. He knows he will be defeated and cast out in the end, but he is determined to take down with him as many others as he possibly can.

So what are some of the devil's tactics in this contest when eternal life is at stake? Here again the experience in the Sacred Grove is instructive. Joseph recorded that in an effort to oppose all that lay ahead, Lucifer exerted "such an astonishing influence over me as to bind my tongue so that I could not speak."[1]

Satan cannot directly take a life. That is one of many things he cannot do. But apparently his effort to stop the work will be reasonably well served if he can just bind the tongue of the faithful. If that is the case, I am looking for Saints young and old who care enough about this battle between good and evil to sign on and speak up. We are at war, and I want to be a one-man recruiting station.

Do you remember the line in the hymn "We Are All Enlisted" about "We are waiting now for soldiers; who'll volunteer?"[2] Of course, the great thing about this call to arms is that we ask *not* for volunteers to fire a rifle or throw a hand grenade. No, we want battalions who will take as their weapons "every word that proceedeth forth from the mouth of God."[3] So I am looking for elders and sisters who will not voluntarily bind their tongues but will, with the Spirit of the Lord and the power of their callings, open their mouths and speak miracles. Such speech, the early Brethren taught, would be the means by which faith's "mightiest works have been, and will be, performed."[4]

I especially ask the young men of the Aaronic Priesthood to sit up and take notice. For you, let me mix in an athletic analogy. This is a life-and-death contest we are in, young men, so I am going to get in your face a little, nose to nose, with just enough fire in my words to singe your eyebrows a little—the way coaches do when the game is close and victory means everything. And with the game on the line, what this coach is telling you is that to play in this match, some of you have to be more morally clean than you now are. In this battle between good and evil, you cannot play for the adversary whenever temptation comes along, and then expect to suit up for the Savior at temple and mission time as if nothing has happened. That, my young friends, you cannot do. God will not be mocked.

So we have a dilemma, you and I. It is that there are thousands of Aaronic Priesthood–age young men already on the records of this Church who constitute our pool of candidates for future missionary service. But the challenge is to have those deacons, teachers, and priests stay active enough and worthy enough to be ordained elders and serve as missionaries. So we need young men—and young women, too—who are already on the team to *stay* on it and stop dribbling out of bounds just when we need you to get in the game and play your hearts out! In almost all athletic contests of which I know, there are lines drawn on the floor or field within which every participant must stay in order to compete. Well, the Lord has drawn lines of worthiness for those called to labor with Him in this work. No missionary can be unrepentant of sexual transgression or profane language or pornographic indulgence and then expect to challenge others to repent of those very things! You can't do that. The Spirit will not be with you, and the words will choke in your throat as you speak them. You cannot travel down what Lehi called "forbidden paths"[5] and expect to guide others to the "strait and narrow"[6] one—it can't be done.

But there is an answer to this challenge for you every bit as much as there is for that investigator to whom you will go. Whoever you are and whatever you have done, you can be forgiven. Every one of you can leave behind any transgression with which you may struggle. It is the miracle of forgiveness; it is the miracle of the Atonement of the Lord Jesus Christ. But you cannot do it without an active commitment to the gospel, and you cannot do it without repentance where it is needed. I am asking you to be active and be clean. If required, I am asking you to *get* active and *get* clean.

Now, we speak boldly to you because anything more subtle doesn't seem to work. We speak boldly because Satan is a real being set on destroying you, and you face his influence at a younger and younger age. So we grab you by the lapels and shout as forcefully as we know how: *"Hark! the sound of battle sounding loudly and clear; Come join the ranks! Come join the ranks!"*[7] My young friends, we need tens of thousands more missionaries in the months and years that lie ahead. They must come from an increased percentage of young people who will be active, clean, and worthy to serve.

To those of you who have served or are now serving, we thank you for the good you have done and for the lives you have touched. Bless you! We also recognize that there are some who have hoped all their lives to serve missions, but for health reasons or other impediments beyond their control, they cannot do so. We publicly and proudly salute this group. We know of your desires, and we applaud your devotion. You have our love and our admiration. You are "on the team" and you always will be, even as you are honorably excused from full-time service. But we need the rest of you!

Now, you fathers and mothers, don't smile and settle back into the comfort of your seats. I am not through here. We need thousands more couples serving in the missions of the Church. Every mission president pleads for them. Everywhere they serve, our couples bring a maturity to the work that no number of nineteen-year-olds, however good they are, can provide. For good and sufficient health, family, or economic reasons, some of you, we realize, may not be able to go just now or perhaps ever. But with a little planning many of you can go.

You can leave your recliner and the remote control for a few short months—and yes, you can leave the grandchildren. Those little darlings will be just fine, and I promise you will do things for them in the service of the Lord that, worlds without end, you could never do if you stayed home to hover over them. What greater gift could grandparents give their posterity than to say by deed as well as word, "In this family we serve missions!"

Missionary work isn't the only thing we need to do in this big, wide, wonderful Church. But almost everything else we need to do depends on people first hearing the gospel of Jesus Christ and coming into the faith. Surely that is why Jesus's final charge to the Twelve was just that basic—to "go ye therefore, and teach all nations, baptizing them in the name of the Father, and of the Son, and of the Holy Ghost."[8] Then, and only then, can the rest of the blessings of the gospel fully come—family solidarity, youth programs, priesthood promises, and ordinances flowing right up to the temple. But as Nephi testified, none of that can come until one has "enter[ed] into the . . . gate."[9] With all that there is to do along the path to eternal life, we need a lot more missionaries opening that gate and helping people through it.

From every Latter-day Saint, young and old, I ask for a stronger and more devoted voice, a voice not only against evil and him who is the personification of it, but a voice for good, a voice for the gospel, a voice for God. Brothers and sisters of all ages, unbind your tongues and watch your words work wonders in the lives of those who are only "kept from the truth because they know not where to find it."[10] *"Haste to the battle, quick to the field; Truth is our helmet, buckler, and shield. Stand by our colors; proudly they wave! We're joyfully, joyfully marching to our home."*[11]

NOTES

From a talk given at the priesthood session of general conference, October 2011.

1. Joseph Smith—History 1:15.
2. "We Are All Enlisted," *Hymns of The Church of Jesus Christ of Latter-day Saints* (1985), no. 250.
3. Doctrine and Covenants 84:44; see also Deuteronomy 8:3; Matthew 4:4.
4. *Lectures on Faith* (1985), 73.
5. 1 Nephi 8:28.
6. 2 Nephi 31:18.
7. "We Are All Enlisted," *Hymns,* no. 250.
8. Matthew 28:19.
9. 2 Nephi 33:9.
10. Doctrine and Covenants 123:12.
11. "We Are All Enlisted," *Hymns,* no. 250.

We no longer think of Zion as *where* we are going to live; we think of it as *how* we are going to live.

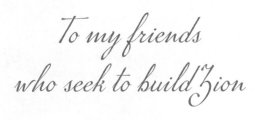

*To my friends
who seek to build Zion*

CHAPTER 9

"ISRAEL, ISRAEL, GOD IS CALLING"

The hymn "Israel, Israel, God Is Calling" is one of the great classics of the Restoration and provides the framework for much of what I want to say here. We could have added "Ye Elders of Israel" for the same purpose. I love hearing the elders and sisters around the world cry out, "O Babylon, O Babylon, we bid thee farewell; we're going to the mountains of Ephraim to dwell."[1] The message of those two hymns is essentially the same—that God is *always* calling the children of Israel to a place where, ultimately, all will be well.

> *Israel, Israel, God is calling,*
> *Calling thee from lands of woe.*
> *Babylon the great is falling;*

God shall all her tow'rs o'erthrow. . . .
Come to Zion, come to Zion,
And within her walls rejoice. . . .
Come to Zion, come to Zion!
Zion's walls shall ring with praise.[2]

In effect, this has been Israel's history down through the ages. When things got too sinful, or there was too much secularization in society, or life with the Gentiles was destroying the moral code and commandments God had given, the children of the covenant would be sent fleeing into the wilderness to reestablish Zion and start all over again.

In Old Testament times Abraham, the father of this kind of covenant, had to flee for his life from Chaldea—literally Babylonia—in his quest for a consecrated life in Canaan (what we would now call the Holy Land).[3] It wasn't many generations before the descendants of Abraham (and then Isaac and Jacob)—by then full-fledged Israelites—lost their Zion and were in bondage in far-off, pagan Egypt.[4] So Moses had to be raised up to lead the children of promise into the wilderness again—this time in the middle of the night, without even time for their bread dough to rise! "Israel, Israel, God is speaking," they undoubtedly sang in their own way. "Hear your great Deliv'rer's voice!"[5]

Not many centuries later, a story of special interest to us unfolded when one of those Israelite families, headed by a prophet named Lehi, was commanded to flee even beloved Jerusalem because, alas, Babylon was again at the door.[6] Here we go again! Little did they know that they were going to an entirely new continent to establish a whole new concept of Zion,[7] but so it would be. And little did they know that it had already happened just like this once before with a group of their forefathers called the Jaredites.[8]

Recognizing that ours is an increasingly international Church, I believe it is still of interest to all who celebrate the Restoration of the gospel that the colonization of America was born of a group fleeing from their former homelands in order to worship as they wished. A distinguished scholar of the Puritan settlement in America described this experience as Christianity's "errand into the wilderness," the effort of modern Israelites to free themselves of Old World godlessness and once again seek the ways of heaven in a new land.[9]

I remind you of one last flight, the flight for which the hymn I have cited was actually written. It was that of our own Church, led by our own prophets, leading our own religious ancestors. With Joseph Smith being hounded through the states of New York, Pennsylvania, Ohio, and Missouri, and being finally murdered in Illinois, we were to see the latter-day reenactment of Israel's children again seeking for a place of seclusion. Brigham Young, the American Moses, as he has been admiringly called, led the Saints to the valleys of the mountains as those foot-weary Saints sang:

> We'll find the place which God for us prepared,
> Far away in the West,

Where none shall come to hurt or make afraid;
There the Saints will be blessed.[10]

Zion. The promised land. The New Jerusalem. Where is it? Well, we are not sure, but we will find it. For more than four thousand years of covenantal history, this has been the pattern: Flee and seek. Run and settle. Escape Babylon. Build Zion's protective walls.

Until now. Until this our day.

One of the many unique characteristics of our dispensation, the dispensation of the fulness of times—the last and greatest of all dispensations—is the changing nature of how we establish the kingdom of God on earth. You see, one of the truly exciting things about this dispensation is that it is a time of mighty, accelerated change. And one thing that has changed is that the Church of God will never again flee. It will never again leave Ur in order to leave Haran, in order to leave Canaan, in order to leave Jerusalem, in order to leave England, in order to leave Kirtland, in order to leave Nauvoo, in order to go who knows where. No, as Brigham Young said for us all, "We have been kicked out of the frying-pan into the fire, out of the fire into the middle of the floor, and here we are and here we will stay."[11]

Of course, that statement wasn't a comment about the Salt Lake Valley only or even the Wasatch Front generally; it became a statement for the members of the Church all over the world. In these last days, in this our dispensation, we would become mature enough to stop running. We would become mature enough to plant our feet and our families and our foundations in every nation, kindred, tongue, and people *permanently.* Zion would be everywhere—wherever the Church is. And with that change—one of the mighty changes of the last days—we no longer think of Zion as *where* we are going to live; we think of it as *how* we are going to live.

To frame this new task just a little, I wish to draw upon three incidents Sister Holland and I have experienced within the fairly recent past.

Incident number one: A few years ago a young friend of mine—a returned missionary—was on one of the college basketball teams in Utah. He was a great young man and a very good ballplayer, but he wasn't playing as much as he hoped he would. His particular talents and skills weren't exactly what that team needed at that stage of its development or his. That happens in athletics. So, with the full support and best wishes of his coaches and his teammates, my young friend transferred to another school where he hoped he might contribute a little more.

As fate would have it, things clicked at the new school, and my friend soon became a starter. And wouldn't you know it—the schedule (determined years before these events transpired) had this young man returning to play against his former team in Salt Lake City's then-named Delta Center.

What happened in that game has bothered me to this day. The vitriolic abuse that poured out of the stands on this young man's head that night—a Latter-day Saint, returned missionary, newlywed who paid his tithing, served in the elders quorum, gave charitable service to the youth in his community, and waited excitedly for a new baby coming to him and his wife—what was said and done and showered upon him that night, and on his wife and their families, should not have been experienced by any human being anywhere, anytime, whatever his sport, whatever his university, or whatever his personal decisions had been about either of them.

But here is the worst part. The coach of this visiting team, something of a legend in the profession, turned to him after a spectacular game and said: "What is going on here? You are the hometown boy who has made good. These are your people. These are your friends." But worst of all, he then said in total bewilderment, "Aren't most of these people members of your church?"

Incident number two: I was invited to speak in a stake single-adult devotional—one of those open-ended "eighteen-and-over" sort of things. As I entered the rear door of the stake center, a thirty-something young woman entered the building at about the same time. Even in the crush of people moving toward the chapel, it was hard not to notice her. As I recall, she had a couple of tattoos, a variety of ear and nose rings, spiky hair reflecting all the colors now available in snow cones, a skirt that was too high, and a blouse that was too low.

Two questions leapt to my mind: Was this woman a struggling soul, not of our faith, who had been led—or even better, had been brought by someone—to this devotional under the guidance of the Lord in an effort to help her find the peace and the direction of the gospel that she needed in her life? Another possibility: Was she a member who had strayed a bit maybe from some of the hopes and standards that the Church encourages for its members but who, thank heaven, was still affiliating and had chosen to attend this Church activity that night?

Incident number three: While participating in the dedication of the Kansas City Missouri Temple, Sister Holland and I were hosted by Brother Isaac Freestone, a police officer by profession and a wonderful high priest in the Liberty Missouri Stake. In our conversations he told us that late one evening he was called to investigate a complaint in a particularly rough part of the city. Over the roar of loud music and with the smell of marijuana in the air, he found one woman and several men drinking and profaning, all of them apparently totally oblivious of the five little children—aged about two through eight years of age—huddled together in one room, trying to sleep on a filthy floor with no bed, no mattress, no pillows, no anything. Brother Freestone looked in the kitchen cupboards and in the refrigerator to see if he could find a single can or carton or box of food of any kind—but he literally could find nothing. He said the dog barking in the backyard had more food than those children did.

In the mother's bedroom he found a bare mattress, the only one in the house. He hunted until he found some sheets (if you could call them that), put them on the mattress, and tucked all five children into the makeshift bed. With tears in his eyes he then knelt down, offered a prayer to Heavenly Father for their protection, and said good night.

As he arose and walked toward the door, one of the children, about age six, jumped out of bed, ran to him, grabbed him by the hand, and pled, "Will you *please* adopt me?" With more tears in his eyes, he put the child back in bed, then found the stoned mother (the men had long since fled) and said to her: "I will be back tomorrow, and heaven help you if some changes are not evident by the time I walk in this door. And there will be more changes after that. You have my word on it."[12]

What do these three incidents have in common? Not much really, except that they give three tiny, very different real-life examples of Babylon—one personal and as silly as deplorable behavior at a basketball game, one more cultural and indicative of one-on-one challenges with those who live differently than we do, and one very large and very serious matter, with legal implications and history so complex that it would seem to be beyond any individual one of us to address it.

In posing these three challenges, I intentionally did not use sensational cases of sexual transgression or physical violence or pornographic addiction, even though those might strike closer to home than the examples I have used. But you are smart enough to make unspoken applications.

Lesson 1: Never "Check Your Religion at the Door"

First, let's finish the basketball incident. The day after that game, when there was some public reckoning and a call to repentance over the incident, one young man said, in effect: "Listen. We are talking about basketball here, not Sunday School. If you can't stand the heat, get out of the kitchen. We pay good money to see these games. We can act the way we want. We check our religion at the door."

"We check our religion at the door"? Lesson number one for the establishment of Zion in the twenty-first century: You *never* "check your religion at the door." Not ever.

That kind of discipleship cannot be—it is not discipleship at all. As the prophet Alma has taught the young women of the Church to declare every week in their Young Women theme, we are "to stand as witnesses of God at all times and in all things, and in all places that ye may be in,"[13] *not* just some of the time, in a few places, or when our team has a big lead.

"Check your religion at the door"! I was furious.

But let's stay with this for a minute because there is a second lesson on its way. Lesson number two in our quest for Zion is that in my righteous indignation (at least we always say it is righteous) I have to make sure that I don't end up doing exactly what I was accusing this young fan of doing: getting mad, acting stupid, losing my cool, ranting about it, wanting to get my hands on him—preferably around his throat—until, before I know it, *I have checked my religion at the door!* No, *someone* in life, someone in the twenty-first century, someone in all of these situations has to live his or her religion because otherwise all we get is a whole bunch of idiots acting like moral pygmies.

It is easy to be righteous when things are calm and life is good and everything is going smoothly. The test is when there is *real* trial or temptation, when there are pressure and fatigue, anger and fear, or the possibility of *real* transgression. Can we be faithful *then*? That is the question because "Israel, Israel, God is calling." Such integrity is, of course, the majesty of "Father, forgive them; for they know not what they do"[14]— right when forgiving and understanding and being generous about your crucifiers is the *last* thing that anyone less perfect than the Savior of the world would want to do. But we have to try; we have to wish to be strong. Whatever the situation or the provocation or the problem, *no* true disciple of Christ can "check his religion at the door."

Lesson 2: Show Compassion, but Be Loyal to the Commandments

That leads me to the woman with the rainbow hair and the many splendored rings. However one would respond to that young woman, the rule forever is that it has to reflect our religious beliefs and our gospel commitments. Therefore, how we respond in any situation has to make things better, not worse. We can't act or react in such a way that we are guilty of a greater offense than, in this case, she is. That doesn't mean that we don't have opinions, that we don't have standards, that we somehow completely disregard divinely mandated "thou shalts" and "thou shalt nots" in life. But it does mean we have to live those standards and defend those "thou shalts" and "thou shalt nots" in a righteous way to the best of our ability, the way the Savior lived and defended them. And He always did what should have been done to make the situation better—from teaching the truth to forgiving sinners to cleansing the temple. It is no small gift to know how to do such things in the right way!

So, with our new acquaintance of the unusual dress and grooming code, we start, above all, by remembering she is a daughter of God and of eternal worth. We start by remembering that she is someone's daughter here on earth as well and could, under other circumstances, be my daughter. We start by being grateful that she is at a Church activity, not avoiding one. In short, we try to be at *our* best in this situation in a desire to help her be at *her* best. We keep praying silently: What is the right thing to do here? And what is the right thing to say? What *ultimately* will make this situation and her better? Asking these questions and really trying to do what the Savior would do is what I think He meant when He said, "Judge not according to the appearance, but judge righteous judgment."[15]

Having said that, I remind us all that while reaching out to help back a lamb who has strayed, we also have a profound responsibility to the ninety-nine who didn't—and to the wishes and will of the Shepherd. There *is* a sheepfold, and we are all supposed to be in it, to say nothing of the safety and blessings that come to us for being there. This Church can never "dumb down" its doctrine in response to social goodwill or political expediency or any other reason. It is only the high ground of revealed truth that gives us any footing on which to lift another who may feel troubled or forsaken. Our compassion and our love—fundamental characteristics and requirements of our Christianity—must *never* be interpreted as compromising the commandments. As the marvelous George MacDonald once said, in such situations "we are not bound to say all that we [believe], but we are bound not even to look [like] what we do not [believe]."[16]

In this regard—this call for compassion and loyalty to the commandments—there is sometimes a chance for a misunderstanding, especially among young people who may think we are not supposed to judge anything, that we are never to make a value assessment of any kind. We have to help each other with that because the Savior makes it clear that in some situations we *have* to judge, we are under obligation to judge—as when He said, "Give not that which is holy unto the dogs, neither cast ye your pearls before swine."[17] That sounds like a judgment to me. The alternative is to surrender to the moral relativism of a deconstructionist, postmodern world that, pushed far enough, posits that ultimately *nothing* is eternally true or especially sacred and, therefore, no one position on any given issue matters more than any other. And that simply is not true.

In this process of evaluation, we are not called on to *condemn* others, but we are called upon to make decisions every day that reflect judgment—we hope good judgment. Elder Dallin H. Oaks once referred to these kinds of decisions as "intermediate judgments," which we often have to make for our own safety or for the safety of others, as opposed to what he called "final judgments," which can be made only by God, who knows all the facts.[18] (Remember, in the scripture quoted earlier, that the Savior said these are to be "righteous judgments," *not* self-righteous judgments, which is a *very* different thing.)

For example, parents have to exercise good judgment every day regarding the safety and welfare of their children. No one would fault a parent who says children must eat their vegetables or who restricts a child from running into a street roaring with traffic. So why should a parent be faulted who cares, at a little later age, what time those children come home at night, or what the moral and behavioral standards of their friends are, or at what age they date, or whether or not they experiment with drugs or pornography or engage in sexual transgression? No, we are making decisions and taking stands and reaffirming our values—in short, making "intermediate judgments"—all the time, or at least we should be.

When we face such situations in complex social issues in a democratic society, it can be very challenging and, to some, confusing. Young people may ask about this position taken or that policy made by the Church, saying: "Well, we don't believe we should live or behave in such and such a way, but why do we have to make other people do the same? Don't they have their free agency? Aren't we being self-righteous and judgmental, forcing our beliefs on others, demanding that *they* act in a certain way?" In those situations you are going to have to explain sensitively why *some* principles are defended and *some* sins opposed *wherever they are found* because the issues and the laws involved are *not* just social or political but eternal in their consequence. And while not wishing to offend those who believe differently from us, we are even more anxious not to offend God, or as the scripture says, "not offend him who is your lawgiver"[19]—and I *am* speaking here of serious moral laws.

But to make the point, let me use the example of a lesser law. It is a little like a teenager saying, "Now that I can drive, I know I am supposed to stop at a red light, but do we really have to be judgmental and try to get everyone else to stop at red lights? Does *everyone* have to do what we do? Don't others have their agency? Must they behave as we do?" You then have to explain why, yes, we do hope *all* will stop at a red light. And you have to do this *without* demeaning those who transgress or who believe differently than we believe because, yes, they *do* have their moral agency.

There is a wide variety of beliefs in this world, and there is moral agency for all, but no one is entitled to act as if God is mute on these subjects or as if commandments only matter if there is public agreement over them. In the twenty-first century we cannot flee any longer. We are going to have to fight for laws and circumstances and environments that allow the free exercise of religion and our franchise in it. That is one way we can tolerate being in Babylon but not of it.

I know of no more important ability and no greater integrity for us to demonstrate in a world from which we cannot flee than to walk that careful path—taking a moral stand according to what God has declared and the laws He has given, but doing it compassionately and with understanding and great charity. Talk about a hard thing to do—to distinguish perfectly between the sin and the sinner. I know of few distinctions that are harder to make, or at least harder to articulate, but we must lovingly try to do exactly that. Believe me, in the world into which we are moving, we are going to have a lot of opportunity to develop such strength, display such courage, and demonstrate such compassion—all at the same time. And I am not speaking now of punk hairdos or rings in your nose.

Lesson 3: Use Gospel Values to Benefit Communities and Countries

Now lastly, the difficult story from Kansas City. Not many of us are going to be police officers or social service agents or judges sitting on a legal bench, but all of us should care for the welfare of others and the moral safety of our extended communities. Elder Quentin L. Cook of the Quorum of the Twelve devoted an entire general conference talk to this subject. In speaking of the need for us to influence society beyond the walls of our own home, he said:

"In addition to protecting our own families, we should be a source of light in protecting our communities. The Savior said, 'Let your light so shine before men, that they may see your good works, and glorify your Father which is in heaven.' . . .

"In our increasingly unrighteous world, it is essential that values based on religious belief be [evident in] . . . the public square. . . .

"Religious faith is a store of light, knowledge, and wisdom and benefits society in a dramatic way."[20]

If we *don't* take gospel blessings to our communities and our countries, the simple fact of the matter is we will never have enough policemen—there will never be enough Isaac Freestones—to enforce moral behavior even if it were enforceable. And it isn't. Those children in that home without food or clothing are sons and daughters of God. That mother, more culpable because she is older and should be more responsible, is also a daughter of God. Such situations may require tough love in formal, even legal ways, but we must try to help when and where we can because we are not checking our religion at the door, even as pathetic and irresponsible as some doors are.

We aren't going to solve every personal or social problem in the world in one day. There will always be poverty, ignorance and transgression, unemployment and abuse, violence and heartache in our neighborhoods and cities and nations. No, we can't do everything, but as the old saying goes, we can do something. And in answer to God's call, the children of Israel are the ones to do it—not to flee Babylon this time but to attack it. Without being naive or Pollyannaish about it, we can live our religion so broadly and unfailingly that we find all kinds of opportunities to help families, bless neighbors, and protect others, including the rising generation.

Latter-day Saints are called upon to be the leaven in the

loaf, the salt that never loses its savor, the light set upon a hill never to be hidden under a bushel. If we do right and talk right and reach out generously with our words *and* our deeds, then when the Savior cuts short His work in righteousness, says time is no more in this last, great dispensation, and then comes in His glory, He will find us—you and me and all of us—doing our best, trying to live the gospel, trying to improve our lives and our Church and our society the best way we can. When He comes, I *so* want to be caught living the gospel. I want to be surprised right in the act of spreading the faith and doing something good. I want the Savior to say to me: "Jeffrey"—because He knows all of our names—"I recognize you not by your title but by your life, the way you are trying to live and the standards you are trying to defend. I see the integrity of your heart. I know you have tried to make things better first and foremost by being better yourself, and then by declaring my word and defending my gospel to others in the most compassionate way you could.

"I know you weren't always successful," He will certainly say, "with your own sins or the circumstances of others, but I believe you honestly tried. I believe in your heart you truly loved me."

I want to have something like that encounter someday as I want nothing else in this mortal life. And I want it for you. I want it for us all. Israel, Israel, God is calling—calling us to live the gospel of Jesus Christ personally in small ways as well as large, and then to reach out to those who may not look or dress or behave quite like we do, and then (where you can) go beyond that to serve in the widest community you can address.

I love the Lord Jesus Christ, whose servant I am trying to be. And I love our Heavenly Father, who cared enough to give Him to us. I know that, regarding that gift, God is calling to Israel in these latter days and that He expects us to respond to that call and to be more Christlike, to be more holy than we now are in our determination to live the gospel and establish Zion. I also know that He will give us both the strength *and* the holiness to be true disciples if we plead for it.

NOTES

From a talk given September 9, 2012, at a Church Educational System devotional.

1. "Ye Elders of Israel," *Hymns of the Church of Jesus Christ of Latter-day Saints* (1985), no. 319.
2. "Israel, Israel, God Is Calling," *Hymns,* no. 7.
3. See Abraham 2:3.
4. See Exodus 1:7–14.
5. "Israel, Israel, God Is Calling," *Hymns,* no. 7.
6. See 1 Nephi 2:2.
7. See 1 Nephi 18:22–24.
8. See Ether 6:5–13.
9. See Perry Miller, *Errand into the Wilderness* (1984), 2–3.
10. "Come, Come, Ye Saints," *Hymns,* no. 30.
11. Brigham Young, quoted in James S. Brown, *Life of a Pioneer* (1971), 121.
12. Isaac Freestone, experience shared with the author on May 5, 2012.
13. Mosiah 18:9.
14. Luke 23:34.
15. John 7:24.
16. George MacDonald, *The Unspoken Sermons* (2011), 264.

17. Matthew 7:6.

18. See Dallin H. Oaks, "'Judge Not' and Judging," *Ensign*, August 1999, 6–13.

19. Doctrine and Covenants 64:13.

20. Quentin L. Cook, "Let There Be Light!" *Ensign*, November 2010, 28–29.

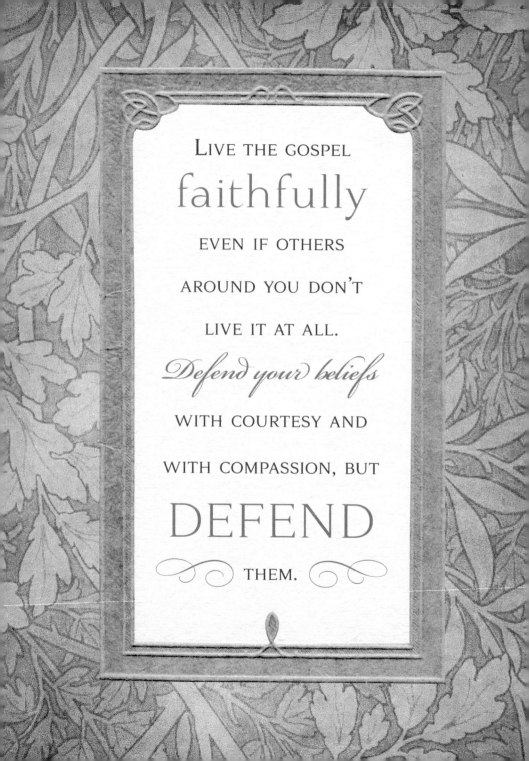

LIVE THE GOSPEL

faithfully

EVEN IF OTHERS

AROUND YOU DON'T

LIVE IT AT ALL.

Defend your beliefs

WITH COURTESY AND

WITH COMPASSION, BUT

DEFEND

THEM.

*To my friends who wish
to be true disciples of Christ*

⟶

CHAPTER 10

THE COST—AND BLESSINGS—
OF DISCIPLESHIP

With admiration and encouragement for everyone who
will need to remain steadfast in these latter days, I say to all
and especially the youth of the Church that if you haven't already, you will one day find yourself called upon to defend
your faith or perhaps even endure some personal abuse simply
because you are a member of The Church of Jesus Christ of
Latter-day Saints. Such moments will require both courage and
courtesy on your part.

For example, a sister missionary recently wrote to me: "My
companion and I saw a man sitting on a bench in the town
square eating his lunch. As we drew near, he looked up and
saw our missionary name tags. With a terrible look in his eye,

he jumped up and raised his hand to hit me. I ducked just in time, only to have him spit his food all over me and start swearing the most horrible things at us. We walked away saying nothing. I tried to wipe the food off of my face, only to feel a clump of mashed potato hit me in the back of the head. Sometimes it is hard being a missionary because right then I wanted to go back, grab that little man, and say, 'EXCUSE ME!' But I didn't."

To this devoted missionary I say, dear child, you have in your own humble way stepped into a circle of very distinguished women and men who have, as the Book of Mormon prophet Jacob said, "view[ed Christ's] death, and suffer[ed] his cross and [borne] the shame of the world."[1]

Indeed, of Jesus Himself, Jacob's brother Nephi wrote: "And the world, because of their iniquity, shall judge him to be a thing of naught; wherefore they scourge him, and he suffereth it; and they smite him, and he suffereth it. Yea, they spit upon him, and he suffereth it, because of his loving kindness and his long-suffering towards the children of men."[2]

In keeping with the Savior's own experience, there has been a long history of rejection and a painfully high price paid by prophets and apostles, missionaries and members in every generation—all those who have tried to honor God's call to lift the human family to "a more excellent way."[3]

"And what shall I more say [of them]?" the writer of the book of Hebrews asks.

"[They] who . . . stopped the mouths of lions,

"Quenched the violence of fire, escaped the edge of the sword, . . . waxed valiant in fight, turned [armies] to flight . . .

"[Saw] their dead raised to life [while] others were tortured, . . .

"And . . . had trial of cruel mockings and scourgings, . . . of bonds and imprisonment:

"They were stoned, . . . were sawn asunder, were tempted, were slain with the sword: . . . wandered about in sheepskins and goatskins; being destitute, afflicted, [and] tormented;

"([They] of whom the world was not worthy:) . . . wandered in deserts, and in mountains, and in dens and caves of the earth."[4]

Surely the angels of heaven wept as they recorded this cost of discipleship in a world that is often hostile to the commandments of God. The Savior Himself shed His own tears over those who for hundreds of years had been rejected and slain in His service. And now He was being rejected and about to be slain.

"O Jerusalem, Jerusalem," Jesus cried, "thou that killest the prophets, and stonest them which are sent unto thee, how often would I have gathered thy children together, even as a hen gathereth her chickens under her wings, and ye would not!

"Behold, your house is left unto you desolate."[5]

And therein lies a message for every young man and young woman in this Church. You may wonder if it is worth it to take a courageous moral stand in high school or to go on a mission only to have your most cherished beliefs reviled or to strive against much in society that sometimes ridicules a life of religious devotion. Yes, it is worth it, because the alternative is to have our "houses" left unto us "desolate"—desolate individuals, desolate families, desolate neighborhoods, and desolate nations.

So here we have the burden of those called to bear the messianic message. In addition to teaching, encouraging, and cheering people on (that is the pleasant part of discipleship), from time to time these same messengers are called upon to worry, to warn, and sometimes just to weep (that is the painful part of discipleship). They know full well that the road leading to the promised land "flowing with milk and honey"[6] of necessity runs by way of Mount Sinai, flowing with "thou shalts" and "thou shalt nots."[7]

Unfortunately, messengers of divinely mandated commandments are often no more popular today than they were anciently, as at least two spit-upon, potato-spattered sister missionaries can now attest. *Hate* is an ugly word, yet there are those today who would say with the corrupt Ahab, "I hate [the prophet Micaiah]; for he never prophesied good unto me, but always [prophesied] evil."[8] That kind of hate for a prophet's honesty cost Abinadi his life. As he said to King Noah: "Because I have told you the truth ye are angry with me. . . . Because I have spoken the word of God ye have judged me that I am mad"[9] or, we might add, provincial, patriarchal, bigoted, unkind, narrow, outmoded, and elderly.

It is as the Lord Himself lamented to the prophet Isaiah:

"[These] children . . . will not hear the law of the Lord:

"[They] say to the seers, See not; and to the prophets, Prophesy not unto us right things, speak unto us smooth things, prophesy deceits:

"Get you out of the way, turn aside out of the path, cause the Holy One of Israel to cease from before us."[10]

Sadly enough, it is a characteristic of our age that if people want any gods at all, they want them to be gods who do not demand much, comfortable gods, smooth gods who not only don't rock the boat but don't even row it, gods who pat us on the head, make us giggle, then tell us to run along and pick marigolds.[11]

Talk about man creating God in his own image! Some-times—and this seems the greatest irony of all—these folks invoke the name of Jesus as one who was this kind of "comfortable" God. Really? He who said not only should we not break commandments, but we should not even *think* about breaking them. And if we do think about breaking them, we have already broken them in our heart. Does that sound like "comfortable" doctrine, easy on the ear and popular down at the village love-in?

And what of those who just want to look at sin or touch it from a distance? Jesus said with a flash, if your eye offends you, pluck it out. If your hand offends you, cut it off.[12] "I came not to [bring] peace, but a sword,"[13] He warned those who thought He spoke only soothing platitudes. No wonder that, sermon after sermon, the local communities "pray[ed] him to depart out of their coasts."[14] No wonder, miracle after miracle, His power was attributed not to God but to the devil.[15] It is obvious that the bumper sticker question "What would Jesus do?" will not always bring a popular response.

At the zenith of His mortal ministry, Jesus said, "Love one another, as I have loved you."[16] To make certain they understood exactly what kind of love that was, He said, "If ye love me, keep my commandments"[17] and "whosoever . . . shall break one of [the] least commandments, *and shall teach men so, he shall be* . . . the least in the kingdom of heaven."[18] Christlike love is the greatest need we have on this planet in part because righteousness was always supposed to accompany it. So if love is to be our watchword, as it *must* be, then by the word of Him who is love personified, we must forsake transgression and any hint of advocacy for it in others. Jesus clearly understood what many in our modern culture seem to forget: that there is a crucial difference between the commandment to forgive sin (which He had an infinite capacity to do) and the warning against condoning it (which He never ever did even once).

Friends, especially my young friends, take heart. Pure Christlike love flowing from true righteousness can change the world. Be strong. Live the gospel faithfully even if others around you don't live it at all. Defend your beliefs with courtesy and with compassion, but defend them. A long history of inspired voices point you toward the path of Christian discipleship. It is a strait path, and it is a narrow path without a great deal of latitude at some points, but it can be thrillingly and successfully traveled, "with . . . steadfastness in Christ, . . . a perfect brightness of hope, and a love of God and of all men."[19] In courageously pursuing such a course, you will forge unshakable faith, you will find safety against ill winds that blow, even shafts in the whirlwind, and you will feel the rock-like strength of our Redeemer, upon whom if you build your unflagging discipleship, you *cannot* fall.[20]

NOTES

From a talk given at general conference, April 2014.

1. Jacob 1:8.
2. 1 Nephi 19:9.
3. 1 Corinthians 12:31; Ether 12:11.
4. Hebrews 11:32–38.
5. Matthew 23:37–38.
6. Exodus 3:8.
7. See Exodus 20:3–17.
8. 2 Chronicles 18:7.
9. Mosiah 13:4.
10. Isaiah 30:9–11.
11. See Henry Fairlie, *The Seven Deadly Sins Today* (1978), 15–16.
12. See Matthew 5:29–30.
13. Matthew 10:34.
14. Mark 5:17.
15. See Matthew 9:34.
16. John 15:12.
17. John 14:15.
18. Matthew 5:19; emphasis added.
19. 2 Nephi 31:20.
20. See Helaman 5:12.

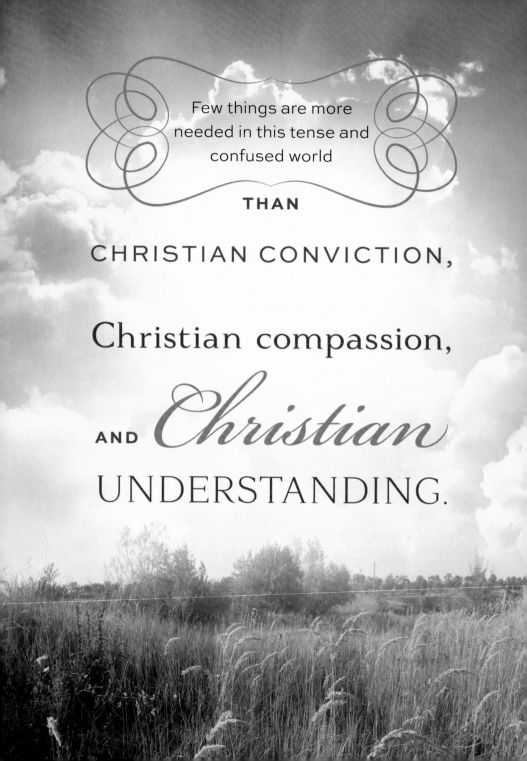

Few things are more needed in this tense and confused world

THAN

CHRISTIAN CONVICTION,

Christian compassion,

AND *Christian* UNDERSTANDING.

*To my friends
of other faiths*

———∽———

CHAPTER 11

STANDING TOGETHER
FOR THE CAUSE OF CHRIST

In addressing friends of other faiths, my purpose is not to make some sort of ecumenical statement. We all are who we are, and we believe what we believe. In saying that, I acknowledge at the outset important doctrinal differences between us. But I also acknowledge that what we have in common is so good, so extensive, and so potentially powerful in addressing the ills of society that we ought in the fellowship of Christ to know and understand each other better than we do.

Friends, you know what I know—that there is in the modern world so much sin and moral decay affecting everyone, especially the young, and it seems to be getting worse by the day. You and I share so many concerns about the spread of pornography and poverty, abuse and abortion, illicit sexual transgression (both heterosexual and homosexual), violence, crudity, cruelty, and temptation, all glaring as close as your daughter's cell phone or your son's iPad. Surely there is a way for people of good will who love God and have taken upon themselves the name of Christ to stand together for the cause of Christ and against the forces of sin. In this we have every right to be bold and believing, for "if God be for us, who can be against us?" You serve and preach, teach and labor in that confidence, and so do I. And in doing so I believe we can trust in that next verse from Romans as well, "He that spared not his own Son, but delivered him up for us all, how shall he not with him also freely give us all things?" I truly believe that if across the world we can all try harder *not* to separate *each other* "from the love of Christ," we will be "more than conquerors through him that loved us."[1]

I don't need to tell anyone that Latter-day Saints and other Christians have not always met on peaceful terms. From the time in the early nineteenth century when Joseph Smith came from his youthful revelatory epiphany and made his bold declaration regarding it, our exchanges have too often been anything but cordial. And yet, strangely enough—and I cannot help but believe this to be a part of a divine orchestration of events in these troubled times—LDS and evangelical academics and church figures have been drawn together since the late 1990s in what I think has become a provocative and constructive theological dialogue. It has been an honest effort to understand and be understood, an endeavor to dispel myths and misrepresentations on *both* sides, a labor of love in which the participants have felt motivated by and moved upon with a quiet force deeper and more profound than a typical interfaith exchange.

The first of those formal dialogues took place in the spring of 2000 at Brigham Young University in Provo, Utah, where, in an earlier life, I served as president. Names and faces have changed somewhat over the years since then, but the dialogue has continued.

Over the next decade the various participants came prepared (through readings of articles and books) to discuss a number of doctrinal subjects, including the Fall of Man, the Atonement of Jesus Christ, Scripture, Revelation, Grace and Works, Trinity/Godhead, Deification, Authority, and Joseph Smith. The dialogues were held not only at BYU but also at Nauvoo, Illinois; Pasadena, California; Palmyra, New York; Chicago, Illinois; and at regular meetings of the American Academy of Religion.

As the dialogue began to take shape, it was apparent that the participants were searching for a paradigm of some sort, a model, a point of reference—were these to be confrontations? Arguments? Debates? Were they to produce a winner and a loser? Just how candid and earnest were they expected to be? Some of the Latter-day Saints wondered: Do the "other guys" see these conversations as our "tryouts" for a place on the Christian team? Is it a grand effort to "fix" us, to "fix"

Mormonism, to make it more traditionally Christian, more acceptable to skeptical onlookers? In turn some of the evangelicals wondered: Are those "other guys" for real? Or is this just another form of their missionary proselytizing? Is what they are saying an accurate expression of LDS belief? Can a person be a New Testament Christian and yet not subscribe to later creeds which most of traditional Christianity would adopt? A question that continued to come up on both sides was just how much "bad theology" can the grace of God compensate for? Before too long, those kinds of issues became part of the dialogue itself, and in the process, the tension began to dissipate.

My LDS friends tell me that the initial feeling of formality has given way to a much more amiable informality, a true form of brother-and-sisterhood, with a kindness in disagreement, a respect for opposing views, and a feeling of responsibility to truly understand (if not necessarily agree with) those not of one's own faith—a responsibility to represent one's doctrines and practices accurately and grasp that of others in the same way. In the words of my friend Richard Mouw of Fuller Theological Seminary, the dialogues came to enjoy "convicted civility."[2]

Realizing that the Latter-day Saints have quite a different hierarchal and organizational structure than most other Christian churches, no official representative of the Church has participated in these talks, nor have there been any ecclesiastical overtones to them. Like you, we have no desire to compromise our doctrinal distinctiveness or forfeit the beliefs that make us who we are. As our third article of faith makes clear, "We believe that through the Atonement of Christ, all mankind may be saved, by obedience to the laws and ordinances of the Gospel." We believe that the authority to perform those saving ordinances was restored to the earth by divine messengers in the earliest years of The Church of Jesus Christ of Latter-day Saints. That authority to perform those ordinances is one of the crucial foundation stones to—and reasons for— the restoration of the church Christ established. Others may not agree that ours is that church, but we are anxious that others not misunderstand us, not accuse us of beliefs we do *not* hold, and not dismiss out of hand our commitment to Christ and His gospel, to say nothing of demonizing us in the process.

Furthermore, we are always looking for common ground and common partners in the "hands-on" work of the ministry. We would be eager to join hands with our friends of every denomination in a united Christian effort to strengthen families and marriages, to demand more morality in media, to provide humane relief effort in times of natural disasters, to address the ever-present plight of the poor, and to guarantee the freedom of religion that will allow all of us to speak out on matters of Christian conscience regarding the social issues of our time. We have a significant record of working together with others on these foundational issues—as, for example, when we have partnered with Catholic Charities in dozens of joint humanitarian efforts both domestically and internationally. And we look forward to continued efforts to unite our faith with that of all who recognize and cherish the role of religion in our society. Most particularly, we must band together to make certain the day never comes that you or I or any other responsible cleric in this nation is forbidden to preach from the pulpit the doctrine he or she holds to be true. But in light of recent socio-political events and current legal challenges stemming from them, particularly regarding the sanctity of marriage, that day could come unless we act decisively in preventing it.[3] The larger and more united the Christian voice, the more likely we are to carry the day in these matters. In that regard we should remember the Savior's warning that "a house divided against itself" will be a house which finds it "cannot stand" against more united foes pursuing an often unholy agenda.[4]

Building on some of this past history, and desirous that we not disagree where we don't need to disagree, I wish to testify to you, our friends, of the Christ we revere and adore in The Church of Jesus Christ of Latter-day Saints. We believe in the historical Jesus who walked the dusty paths of the Holy Land and declare that He is one and the same God as the Divine Jehovah of the Old Testament. We declare Him to be both fully God in His Divinity and fully human in His mortal experience, the Son who was a God and the God who was a Son; that He is, in the language of the Book of Mormon, "the Eternal God."[5] We testify He is one with the Father and the Holy Ghost, the Three being One:[6] one in spirit, one in strength, one in purpose, one in voice, one in glory, one in will, one in goodness, and one in grace—one in every conceivable form and facet of unity *except* that of their separate physical embodiment. We testify that Christ was born of His divine Father and a virgin mother, that from the age of twelve onward He was about His true Father's business, that in doing so He lived a perfect, sinless life and thus provided a pattern for all who come unto Him for salvation.

In the course of that ministry we bear witness of every sermon He ever gave, every prayer He ever uttered, every miracle He ever called down from heaven, and every redeeming act He ever performed. In this latter regard we testify that in fulfilling the divine plan for our salvation, He took upon Himself all the sins, sorrows, and sicknesses of the world, bleeding at every pore in the anguish of it all, beginning in Gethsemane and dying upon the cross of Calvary as a vicarious offering for those sins and sinners, including for each of us.

Early in the Book of Mormon, a Nephite prophet "saw that [Jesus] was lifted up on the cross and slain for the sins of the world."[7] Later that same Lord affirmed: "Behold, I have given unto you my gospel, and this is the gospel which I have given unto you—that I came into the world to do the will of my Father, because my Father sent me. And my Father sent me that I might be lifted up upon the cross."[8] Indeed, it is a gift of the Spirit "to know that Jesus Christ is the Son of God, and that he was crucified for the sins of the world."[9]

We declare that three days after the Crucifixion He rose from the tomb in glorious immortality, the first fruits of the Resurrection, thereby breaking the physical bands of death and the spiritual bonds of hell, providing an immortal future for both the body and the spirit, a future which can only be realized in its full glory and grandeur by accepting Him and His name as the only "name under heaven given among men, whereby we must be saved." Neither is there nor can there ever be "salvation in any other."[10] We declare that He will come again to earth, this time in might, majesty, and glory, to reign as King of kings and Lord of lords. This is the Christ whom we praise, in whose grace we trust implicitly and explicitly, and who is "the Shepherd and Bishop of [our] souls."[11]

Joseph Smith was once asked the question, "What are the fundamental principles of your religion?" He replied: "The fundamental principles of our religion are the testimony of the Apostles and Prophets, concerning Jesus Christ, that he died, was buried, and rose again the third day, and ascended into heaven; and all other things which pertain to our religion are only appendages to it."[12]

As a rule Latter-day Saints are known as an industrious people, a works-conscious people. For us, the works of righteousness, what we might call "dedicated discipleship," are an unerring measure of the reality of our faith; we believe with James, the brother of Jesus, that true faith always manifests itself in faithfulness.[13] We teach that those Puritans were closer to the truth than they realized when they expected a "godly walk" from those under covenant.

Salvation and eternal life are free;[14] indeed, they are the greatest of all the gifts of God.[15] Nevertheless, we teach that one must qualify to receive those gifts by declaring and demonstrating "faith in the Lord Jesus Christ"—by trusting in and relying upon "the merits, and mercy, and grace of the Holy Messiah,"[16] a phrase taken from the Book of Mormon. For us, the fruits of that faith include repentance, the receipt of gospel covenants and ordinances (including baptism), and a heart of gratitude that motivates us to deny ourselves of all ungodliness, to take up [our] cross daily,[17] and to keep His commandments—*all* of His commandments.[18] We rejoice with the Apostle Paul: "Thanks be to God, [who] giveth us the victory through our Lord Jesus Christ."[19] In that spirit, as one Book of Mormon prophet wrote, "We talk of Christ, we rejoice in Christ, we preach of Christ, we prophesy of Christ . . . that our children may know to what source they may look for a remission of their sins [and] . . . look forward unto that life which is in Christ."[20] I hope this witness which I bear to you and to the world helps you understand something of the inexpressible love we feel for the Savior of the world in The Church of Jesus Christ of Latter-day Saints.

Given our shared devotion to the Lord Jesus Christ and given the challenges we face in our society, to which I alluded earlier and which you are addressing so faithfully, surely we can find a way to unite in a national—or international—call to Christian conscience. Some years ago, Tim LaHaye wrote:

"If religious Americans work together in the name of our mutually shared moral concerns, we just might succeed in re-establishing the civic moral standards that our forefathers thought were guaranteed by the Constitution.

" . . . I really believe that we are in a fierce battle for the very survival of our culture. . . . Obviously I am not suggesting joint evangelistic crusades with these religions; that would reflect an unacceptable theological compromise for all of us. [Nevertheless], all of our nation's religious citizens need to develop a respect for other religious people and their beliefs. We need not accept their beliefs, but we can respect the people and realize that we have more in common with each other than we ever will with the secularizers of this country. It is time for all religiously committed citizens to unite against our common enemy."[21]

To be sure, there is a risk associated with learning something new about someone else. New insights always affect old perspectives, and thus some rethinking, rearranging, and restructuring of our worldviews are inevitable. When we look beyond a man or woman's color or ethnic group or social circle or church or synagogue or mosque or creed or statement of belief, when we try our best to see them for who and what they are, children of the same God, something good and worthwhile happens within us, and we are thereby drawn into a closer union with that God who is the Father of us all.

In reflecting on his visit to Salt Lake City and his major message in our historic Tabernacle on Temple Square in November 2004, Ravi Zacharias observed:

"The last time an Evangelical Christian was invited to speak there was 1899, when D. L. Moody spoke. . . . [Assuming this second visit would not seem too hasty] I accepted the invitation, . . . and I spoke on the exclusivity and sufficiency of Jesus

Christ. I also asked if I could bring my own music, to which they also graciously agreed. So Michael Card joined us to share his music. He did a marvelous job, and one of the pieces he sang brought a predictable smile to all present. It was based on Peter's visit to Cornelius' home and was entitled, 'I'm Not Supposed To Be Here.' He couldn't have picked a better piece! I can truly say that I sensed the anointing of the Lord as I preached and still marvel that the event happened. The power of God's presence, even amid some opposition, was something to experience. As the one closing the meeting said, 'I don't want this evening to end.' Only time will tell the true impact. Who knows what the future will bring? Our faith is foundationally and theologically very different from the Mormon faith, but maybe the Lord is doing something far beyond what we can see."[22]

Few things are more needed in this tense and confused world than Christian conviction, Christian compassion, and Christian understanding. Joseph Smith observed in 1843, less than a year before his death, "If I esteem mankind to be in error, shall I bear them down? No. I will lift them up, and in their own way too, if I cannot persuade them my way is better; and I will not seek to compel any man to believe as I do, only by the force of reasoning, for truth will cut its own way. Do you believe in Jesus Christ and the Gospel of salvation which he revealed? So do I. Christians should cease wrangling and contending with each other, and cultivate the principles of union and friendship in their midst; and they will do it before the millennium can be ushered in and Christ takes possession of His kingdom."[23]

I close with this love for you expressed by two valedictories in our scripture. First this from the New Testament author of Hebrews:

"[May] the God of peace, that brought again from the dead our Lord Jesus, that great shepherd of the sheep, through the blood of the everlasting covenant,

"Make you perfect in every good work to do his will, working in you that which is wellpleasing in his sight, through Jesus Christ; to whom be glory for ever and ever. Amen."[24]

And this from the Book of Mormon, a father writing to his son:

"Be faithful in Christ [and] may [He] lift thee up, and may his sufferings and death . . . and his mercy and long-suffering , and the hope of his glory and of eternal life, rest in your mind forever.

"And may the grace of God the Father, whose throne is high in the heavens, and our Lord Jesus Christ, who sitteth on the right hand of his power, until all things shall become subject unto him, be, and abide with you forever. Amen."[25]

NOTES

From a talk given March 10, 2011, to a national meeting of Christian evangelical leaders held in Salt Lake City.

1. Romans 8: 31, 32, 35, 37.
2. A term introduced in his book, *Uncommon Decency: Christian Civility in an Uncivil World* (Downers Grove, IL: InterVarsity Press, 1992).
3. See the remarks of my fellow Apostle, Elder Dallin Oaks, at Chapman University Law School, "Preserving Religious Freedom," February 4, 2011.

4. See Luke 11:17; Matthew 12:25; Mark 3:25.
5. Title Page, Book of Mormon.
6. 3 Nephi 11:36.
7. 1 Nephi 11:33.
8. 3 Nephi 27:13–14; compare Doctrine and Covenants 76:40–42.
9. Doctrine and Covenants 46:13.
10. Acts 4:12.
11. 1 Peter 2:25.
12. *Teachings of the Prophet Joseph Smith,* sel. Joseph Fielding Smith (1976), 121.
13. James 2.
14. 2 Nephi 2:4.
15. Doctrine and Covenants 6:13; 14:7.
16. 2 Nephi 2:8; 31:19; Moroni 6:4.
17. Luke 9:23.
18. John 14:15.
19. 1 Corinthians 15:57.
20. 2 Nephi 25:26–27.
21. Tim LaHaye, *The Race for the 21st Century* (1986), 109.
22. Ravi Zacharias, *RZIM Newsletter,* vol. 3 (Winter 2004), 2.
23. *Teachings of the Prophet Joseph Smith,* 313–14.
24. Hebrews 13:20–21.
25. Moroni 9:25–26.

Exercise more control

over even the

MARGINAL

MOMENTS

that confront you.

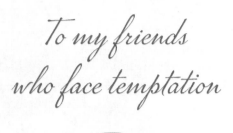

To my friends
who face temptation

CHAPTER 12

A Place No More
for the Enemy of My Soul

As Sister Holland and I recently disembarked at a distant airport, three beautiful young women getting off the same flight hurried up to greet us. They identified themselves as members of the Church, which wasn't too surprising because those not of our faith usually don't rush up to us in airports. In a conversation we hadn't expected, we soon learned through their tears that all three of these women were recently divorced, that in each case their husbands had been unfaithful to them, and in each case the seeds of alienation and transgression had begun with an attraction to pornography.

Perhaps it was the father in me or maybe the grandfather, but the tears in those young women's eyes brought tears to mine and Sister Holland's, and the questions they asked left me asking, "Why is there so much moral decay around us, and why are so many individuals and families, including some in the Church, falling victim to it, being tragically scarred by it?"

But, of course, I knew at least part of the answer to my own question. Most days we all find ourselves assaulted by immoral messages of some kind flooding in on us from every angle. The darker sides of the movie, television, and music industry step further and further into offensive language and sexual misconduct. Tragically, the same computer and Internet service that allow me to do my family history and prepare those names for temple work could, without filters and controls, allow my children or grandchildren access to a global cesspool of perceptions that could blast a crater in their brains forever.

Remember that those young wives said their husbands' infidelity began with an attraction to pornography, but immoral activity is not just a man's problem, and husbands aren't the only ones offending. The compromise available at the click of a mouse—including what can happen in a chat room's virtual encounter—is no respecter of persons, male or female, young or old, married or single. And just to make sure that temptation is ever more accessible, the adversary is busy extending his coverage, as they say in the industry, to cell phones, video games, and MP3 players.

If we stop chopping at the branches of this problem and strike more directly at the root of the tree, not surprisingly we find lust lurking furtively there. *Lust* is an unsavory word, and it is certainly an unsavory topic to address, but there is good reason why in some traditions it is known as the most deadly of the seven deadly sins.[1]

Why is lust such a deadly sin? Well, in addition to the completely Spirit-destroying impact it has upon our souls, I think it is a sin because it defiles the highest and holiest relationship God gives us in mortality—the love that a man and a woman have for each other and the desire that couple has to bring children into a family intended to be forever. Someone said once that true love must include the idea of permanence. True love endures. But lust changes as quickly as it can turn a pornographic page or glance at yet another potential object for gratification walking by, male or female. True love we are absolutely giddy about—as I am about Sister Holland; we shout it from the housetops. But lust is characterized by shame and stealth and is almost pathologically clandestine—the later and darker the hour the better, with a double-bolted door just in case. Love makes us instinctively reach out to God and other people. Lust, on the other hand, is anything but godly and celebrates self-indulgence. Love comes with open hands and open heart; lust comes with only an open appetite.

These are just some of the reasons that prostituting the true meaning of love—either with imagination or another person—is so destructive. It destroys that which is second only to our faith in God—namely, faith in those we love. It shakes the pillars of trust upon which present—or future—love is built, and it takes a long time to rebuild that trust when it is lost. Push that idea far enough—whether it be as personal as a family member or as public as elected officials, business leaders, media stars, and athletic heroes—and soon enough on the building once constructed to house morally responsible societies, we can hang a sign saying, "This property is vacant."[2]

Whether we be single or married, young or old, let's talk for a moment about how to guard against temptation in whatever form it may present itself. We may not be able to cure all of society's ills, but let's speak of what some personal actions can be.

• Above all, start by separating yourself from people, materials, and circumstances that will harm you. As those battling something like alcoholism know, the pull of proximity can be fatal. So too in moral matters. Like Joseph in the presence of Potiphar's wife,[3] just run—run as far away as you can get from whatever or whoever it is that beguiles you. And please, when fleeing the scene of temptation, do *not* leave a forwarding address.

• Acknowledge that people bound by the chains of true addictions often need more help than self-help, and that may include you. Seek that help and welcome it. Talk to your bishop. Follow his counsel. Ask for a priesthood blessing. Use the Church's Family Services offerings or seek other suitable professional help. Pray without ceasing. Ask for angels to help you.

• Along with filters on computers and a lock on affections, remember that the only real control in life is self-control. Exercise more control over even the marginal moments that confront you. If a TV show is indecent, turn it off. If a movie is crude, walk out. If an improper relationship is developing, sever it. Many of these influences, at least initially, may not technically be evil, but they can blunt our judgment, dull our spirituality, and lead to something that could be evil. An old proverb says that a journey of a thousand miles begins with one step,[4] so watch your step.

• Like thieves in the night, unwelcome thoughts can and do seek entrance to our minds. But we don't have to throw open the door, serve them tea and crumpets, and then tell them where the silverware is kept! (You shouldn't be serving tea anyway.) Throw the rascals out! Replace lewd thoughts with hopeful images and joyful memories; picture the faces of those who love you and would be shattered if you let them down. More than one man has been saved from sin or stupidity by remembering the face of his mother, his wife, or his child waiting somewhere for him at home. Whatever thoughts you have, make sure they are welcome in your heart by invitation only. As an ancient poet once said, let will be your reason.[5]

• Cultivate and be where the Spirit of the Lord is. Make sure that includes your own home or apartment, dictating the kind of art, music, and literature you keep there. If you are endowed, go to the temple as often as your circumstances allow. Remember that the temple arms you "with [God's] power, . . . [puts His] glory . . . round about [you], and [gives His] angels . . . charge over [you]."[6] And when you leave the temple, remember the symbols you take with you, never to be set aside or forgotten.

Most people in trouble end up crying, "What was I thinking?" Well, whatever they were thinking, they weren't thinking of Christ. Yet, as members of His Church, we pledge every Sunday of our lives to take upon ourselves His name and promise to "always remember him."[7] So let us work a little harder at remembering Him—especially that He has "borne our griefs, and carried our sorrows . . . , [that] he was bruised for our iniquities . . . ; and with his stripes we are healed."[8] Surely it would guide our actions in a dramatic way if we remembered that every time we transgress, we hurt not only those we love, but we also hurt Him, one who so dearly loves us. But if we do sin, however serious that sin may be, we can be rescued by that same majestic figure, He who bears the only name given under heaven whereby *any* man or woman can be saved.[9] When we are confronting our transgressions and our souls are harrowed up with true pain, may we all echo the repentant Alma and utter his life-changing cry: "O Jesus, thou Son of God, have mercy on me."[10]

I have tried to speak of love—real love, true love, respect for it, the proper portrayal of it in the wholesome societies mankind has known, the sanctity of it between a married man and woman, and the families that love ultimately creates. I've tried to speak of the redeeming manifestation of love, charity personified, which comes to us through the grace of Christ Himself. I have of necessity also spoken of *el diablo,* the diabolical one, the father of lies and lust, who will do anything he can to counterfeit true love, to profane and desecrate true love wherever and whenever he encounters it. And I have spoken of his desire to destroy us if he can.

When we face such temptations in our time, we must declare, as young Nephi did in his, "[I will] give place no more for the enemy of my soul."[11] We can reject the evil one. If we want it dearly and deeply enough, that enemy can and will be rebuked by the redeeming power of the Lord Jesus Christ. Furthermore, I promise you that the light of His everlasting gospel can and will again shine brightly where you feared life had gone hopelessly, helplessly dark. May the joy of our fidelity to the highest and best within us be ours as we keep our love and our marriages, our society and our souls, as pure as they were meant to be.

NOTES

From a talk given at general conference, April 2010.

1. See, for example, Henry Fairlie's excellent *The Seven Deadly Sins Today* (1978).
2. See Fairlie, *The Seven Deadly Sins Today,* 175.
3. See Genesis 39:1–13.
4. Lao Tzu, in John Bartlett, comp., *Bartlett's Familiar Quotations,* 14th ed. (1968), 74.
5. See Juvenal, *The Satires,* satire 6, line 223.
6. Doctrine and Covenants 109:22.
7. Doctrine and Covenants 20:77; see also verse 79.
8. Isaiah 53:4–5.
9. See Acts 4:12.
10. Alma 36:18.
11. 2 Nephi 4:28.

GOD DOESN'T CARE

nearly as much about

where you have been

as He does about

WHERE YOU ARE

and, with His help,

where you are willing

to go.

*To my friends
who want to move forward*

———— ⌒ ————

CHAPTER 13

"REMEMBER LOT'S WIFE"

I want to talk to you about the past and the future, with an eye toward any time of transition and change in your life—and those moments come virtually every day of our lives.

As a scriptural theme for this discussion, I have chosen the second-shortest verse in all of holy scripture. I am told that the shortest verse—a verse that every missionary memorizes and holds ready in case he is called on spontaneously in a zone conference—is John 11:35: "Jesus wept." Here is a second option, another shortie that will dazzle your mission president in case you are called on two zone conferences in a row. It is Luke 17:32, where the Savior cautions, "Remember Lot's wife."

What did He mean by such an enigmatic little phrase? To

find out, I suppose we need to do as He suggested. Let's recall who Lot's wife was.

The original story, of course, comes to us out of the days of Sodom and Gomorrah, when the Lord, having had as much as He could stand of the worst that men and women could do, told Lot and his family to flee because those cities were about to be destroyed. "Escape for thy life," the Lord said, "*look not behind thee* . . . ; escape to the mountain, lest thou be consumed."[1]

With less than immediate obedience and more than a little negotiation, Lot and his family ultimately did leave town, but just in the nick of time. The scriptures tell us what happened at daybreak the morning following their escape: "The Lord rained upon Sodom and upon Gomorrah brimstone and fire from the Lord out of heaven; and he overthrew those cities."[2]

Then our theme comes in the next verse. Surely, surely, with the Lord's counsel "look not behind thee" ringing clearly in her ears, Lot's wife, the record says, "looked back," and she was turned into a pillar of salt.[3]

I am not going to talk about the sins of Sodom and Gomorrah, nor of the comparison the Lord Himself has made to those days and our own time. I am not even going to talk about obedience and disobedience. I just want to talk for little while about looking back and looking ahead.

One of the purposes of history is to teach us the lessons of life. George Santayana, who should be more widely read than he is, is perhaps best known for saying, "Those who cannot remember the past are condemned to repeat it."[4]

So, if history is this important—and it surely is—what did Lot's wife do that was so wrong? As something of a student of history, I have thought about that and offer this as a partial answer. Apparently what was wrong with Lot's wife was that she wasn't just *looking* back; in her heart she wanted to *go* back. It would appear that even before they were past the city limits, she was already missing what Sodom and Gomorrah had offered her. As Elder Neal A. Maxwell once said, such people know they should have their primary residence in Zion, but they still hope to keep a summer cottage in Babylon.[5]

It is possible that Lot's wife looked back with resentment toward the Lord for what He was asking her to leave behind. We certainly know that Laman and Lemuel were resentful when Lehi and his family were commanded to leave Jerusalem. So it isn't just that she looked back; she looked back *longingly*. In short, her attachment to the past outweighed her confidence in the future. That, apparently, was at least part of her sin.

So, as we try to benefit from a proper view of what has gone before, I plead with you not to dwell on days now gone, nor to yearn vainly for yesterdays, however good those yesterdays may have been. The past is to be learned from but not lived in. We look back to claim the embers from glowing experiences but not the ashes. And when we have learned what we need to learn and have brought with us the best that we have experienced, then we look ahead, we remember that *faith is always pointed toward the future.* Faith always has to do with blessings and truths and events that will *yet* be efficacious in our lives. So a more theological way to talk about Lot's wife is to say that she did not have faith. She doubted the Lord's ability to give her something better than she already had. Apparently she thought—fatally, as it turned out—that nothing that lay ahead could possibly be as good as those moments she was leaving behind.

It is here at this moment in this little story that we wish Lot's wife had been a student at BYU enrolled in a freshman English class. With any luck, she might have read, as I did, this verse from Edwin Arlington Robinson:

> *Miniver Cheevy, child of scorn,*
> *Grew lean while he assailed the seasons;*
> *He wept that he was ever born,*
> *And he had reasons.*
>
> *Miniver loved the days of old*
> *When swords were bright and steeds were prancing;*
> *The vision of a warrior bold*
> *Would set him dancing.*
>
> *Miniver sighed for what was not,*
> *And dreamed, and rested from his labors;*
> *He dreamed of Thebes and Camelot,*
> *And Priam's neighbors. . . .*
>
> *Miniver cursed the commonplace*
> *And eyed a khaki suit with loathing;*

He missed the medieval grace
Of iron clothing. . . .

Miniver Cheevy, born too late,
Scratched his head and kept on thinking;
Miniver coughed, and called it fate,
And kept on drinking.[6]

To yearn to go back to a world that cannot be lived in now; to be perennially dissatisfied with present circumstances and have only dismal views of the future; to miss the here-and-now-and-tomorrow because we are so trapped in the there-and-then-and-yesterday—these are some of the sins, if we may call them that, of both Lot's wife and old Mr. Cheevy. (Now, as a passing comment, I don't know whether Lot's wife, like Miniver, was a drinker, but if she was, she certainly ended up with plenty of salt for her pretzels.)

One of my favorite books of the New Testament is Paul's too-seldom-read letter to the Philippians. After reviewing the very privileged and rewarding life of his early years—his birthright, his education, his standing in the Jewish community—Paul says that all of that was nothing ("dung," he calls it) compared to his conversion to Christianity. He says, and I paraphrase: "I have stopped rhapsodizing about 'the good old days' and now eagerly look toward the future 'that I may apprehend that for which Christ apprehended me.'" Then comes this verse:

"This one thing I do, forgetting those things which are behind, and reaching forth unto those things which are before, I press toward the mark for the prize of the high calling of God in Christ Jesus."[7]

No Lot's wife here. No looking back at Sodom and Gomorrah here. Paul knows it is out there in the future, up ahead wherever heaven is taking us, where we will win "the prize of the high calling of God in Christ Jesus."

Let me add a lesson that applies both in your own life and also in the lives of others. There is something in us, at least in too many of us, that particularly fails to forgive and forget earlier mistakes in life—either mistakes we ourselves have made or the mistakes of others. That is not good. It is not Christian. It stands in terrible opposition to the grandeur and majesty of the Atonement of Christ. To be tied to earlier mistakes—our own or other people's—is the worst kind of wallowing in the past from which we are called to cease and desist.

I can't tell you the number of couples I have counseled who, when they are deeply hurt or even just deeply stressed, reach farther and farther into the past to find yet a bigger brick to throw through the window "pain" of their marriage. When something is over and done with, when it has been repented of as fully as it can be repented of, when life has moved on as it should and a lot of other wonderfully good things have happened since then, it is *not* right to go back and open up some ancient wound that the Son of God Himself died trying to heal.

Let people repent. Let people grow. Believe that people can change and improve. Is that faith? Yes! Is that hope? Yes! Is it charity? Yes! Above all, it is charity, the pure love of Christ. If something is buried in the past, leave it buried. Don't keep going back with your little sand pail and beach shovel to dig it up, wave it around, and then throw it at someone, saying, "Hey! Do you remember *this*?" Splat!

Well, guess what? That is probably going to result in some ugly morsel being dug up out of *your* landfill with the reply, "Yeah, I remember it. Do *you* remember *this*?" Splat.

And soon enough everyone comes out of that exchange dirty and muddy and unhappy and hurt, when what God, our Father in Heaven, pleads for is cleanliness and kindness and happiness and healing.

Such dwelling on past lives, including past mistakes, is just not right! It is not the gospel of Jesus Christ. It is worse than Miniver Cheevy, and in some ways worse than Lot's wife, because at least there he and she were only destroying themselves. In these cases of marriage and family and wards and apartments and neighborhoods, we can end up destroying so many, many others.

Perhaps as we contemplate moving forward in the future there is no greater requirement for us than to do as the Lord Himself said He does: "Behold, he who has repented of his sins, the same is forgiven, and I, the Lord, remember them no more."[8] The proviso, of course, is that repentance has to be sincere, but when it is, and when honest effort is being made to progress, we are guilty of the greater sin if we keep remembering and recalling and rebashing someone with their earlier mistakes—and that "someone" might be ourselves. We can be so hard on ourselves, often much more so than with others!

Now, like the Anti-Nephi-Lehies of the Book of Mormon, bury your weapons of war, and leave them buried. Forgive, and do that which is harder than to forgive: Forget. And when it comes to mind again, forget it again.

You can remember just enough to avoid repeating the mistake, but then put the rest of it all on the dung heap Paul spoke of to those Philippians. Dismiss the destructive and keep dismissing it until the beauty of the Atonement of Christ has revealed to you your bright future and the bright future of your family and your friends and your neighbors. God doesn't care nearly as much about where you have been as He does about where you are and, with His help, where you are willing to go. Such is the wonder of faith and repentance and the miracle of the gospel of Jesus Christ. That is the thing Lot's wife didn't get—and neither did Laman and Lemuel and a host of others in the scriptures.

I shared earlier a little verse remembered from one of my BYU English classes. May I move toward a close with a few lines from another favorite poet whom I probably met in that same class or one similar to it. Robert Browning wrote:

> *Grow old along with me!*
> *The best is yet to be,*
> *The last of life, for which the first was made:*
> *Our times are in His hand*

Who saith, "A whole I planned,
Youth shows but half; trust God: see all, nor be afraid!" [9]

Sister Holland and I were married about the time both of us were reading poems like that in BYU classrooms. We had absolutely no money. Zero. For a variety of reasons, neither of our families was able to help finance our education. We had a small apartment just south of campus—the smallest we could find: two rooms and a half bath. We were both working too many hours trying to stay afloat financially, but we had no other choice.

I remember one fall day—I think it was in the first semester after our marriage in 1963—we were walking together up the hill past the Maeser Building on the sidewalk that led between the President's Home and the Brimhall Building. Somewhere on that path we stopped and wondered what we had gotten ourselves into. Life that day seemed so overwhelming, and the undergraduate plus graduate years that we still anticipated before us seemed monumental, nearly insurmountable. Our love for each other and our commitment to the gospel were strong, but most of all the other temporal things around us seemed particularly ominous.

On a spot that I could probably still mark for you today, I turned to Pat and said something like this: "Honey, should we give up? I can get a good job and carve out a good living for us. I can do some things. I'll be okay without a degree. Should we stop trying to tackle what right now seems so difficult to face?"

In my best reenactment of Lot's wife, I said, in effect, "Let's go back. Let's go home. The future holds nothing for us."

Then my beloved little bride did what she has done for five decades since then. She grabbed me by the lapels and said, "We are not going back. We are not going home. The future holds *everything* for us."

She stood there in the sunlight that day and gave me a real talk. I don't recall that she quoted Paul, but there was certainly plenty in her voice that said she was committed to setting aside all that was past in order to "press toward the mark" and seize the prize of God that lay yet ahead. It was a living demonstration of faith. It was "the substance of things hoped for, the evidence of things not seen."[10] So we laughed, kept walking, and finished up sharing a root beer—one glass, two straws—at the then newly constructed Wilkinson Center.

Twenty years later I would, on occasion, look out of the window of the President's Home across the street from the Brimhall Building and picture there on the sidewalk two newlywed BYU students, down on their money and down even more on their confidence. And as I would gaze out that window, usually at night, I would occasionally see not Pat and Jeff Holland but others walking that same sidewalk. I would see them sometimes as couples, sometimes as a group of friends, sometimes as just a lone student. I knew something of what those people were feeling. Some of you might be having similar thoughts: Is there any future for me? Will I be safe? Will life be sound? Can I trust in the Lord and in the future? Or would it be better to look back, to go back, to go home?

To all such of every generation, I call out, "Remember Lot's wife." Faith is for the future. Faith builds on the past but never longs to stay there. Faith trusts that God has great things in store for each of us and that Christ truly is the "high priest of good things to come."[11]

Keep your eyes on your dreams, however distant and far away. Live to see the miracles of repentance and forgiveness, of trust and divine love that will transform your life today, tomorrow, and forever.

NOTES

From a talk given January 13, 2009, at a Brigham Young University devotional.

1. Genesis 19:17; emphasis added.
2. Genesis 19:24–25.
3. Genesis 19:26.
4. George Santayana, *Reason in Common Sense,* vol. 1 of *The Life of Reason* (1905–1906).
5. See Larry W. Gibbons, "Wherefore, Settle This in Your Hearts," *Ensign,* November 2006, 102; also Neal A. Maxwell, *A Wonderful Flood of Light* (1990), 47.
6. Edwin Arlington Robinson, "Miniver Cheevy" (1910), stanzas 1–3, 6, 8.
7. Philippians 3:13–14.
8. D&C 58:42.
9. Robert Browning, "Rabbi Ben Ezra" (1864), stanza 1.
10. Hebrews 11:1.
11. Hebrews 9:11.

You make

the gospel of

JESUS CHRIST

what it is—

a living reminder

of His grace

and mercy.

To my friends
for whom I am so grateful

CHAPTER 14

BECAUSE OF YOUR FAITH

We all know there are special keys, covenants, and responsibilities given to the presiding officers of the Church. This is why we sing, rightfully, "We thank thee, O God, for a prophet." But we also know that the Church draws incomparable strength, a truly unique vitality, from the faith and devotion of *every* member, whoever you may be. Not one of us among the Brethren could serve without your prayers and without your support. Your loyalty and your love mean more to us than we can ever possibly say.

In that spirit, I wish to say that *we* sustain *you,* that we return to *you* those same heartfelt prayers and that same expression of love. In whatever country you live, however young or inadequate you feel, or however aged or limited you see yourself as being, I testify you are individually loved of God, you are central to the meaning of His work, and you are cherished and prayed for by the presiding officers of His Church. The personal value, the sacred splendor of every *one* of you is the very reason there is a plan for salvation and exaltation. Contrary to the parlance of the day, this *is* about *you*.

I have struggled to find an adequate way to tell you how loved of God you are and how grateful we are for you. I am trying to be voice for the very angels of heaven in thanking you for every good thing you have ever done, for every kind word you have ever said, for every sacrifice you have ever made in extending to someone—to anyone—the beauty and blessings of the gospel of Jesus Christ.

I am grateful for Young Women leaders who go to girls camp and, without shampoo, showers, or mascara, turn smoky, campfire testimony meetings into some of the most riveting spiritual experiences those girls—or those leaders—will experience in their lifetime. I am grateful for *all* the women of the Church who in my life have been as strong as Mount Sinai and as compassionate as the Mount of Beatitudes. We smile sometimes about our sisters' stories—you know, green Jell-O, quilts, and funeral potatoes. But my family has been the grateful recipient of each of those items at one time or another—and in one case, the quilt and the funeral potatoes on the same day. It was just a small quilt—tiny, really—to make my deceased baby brother's journey back to his heavenly home as warm and comfortable as our Relief Society sisters wanted him to be. The food provided for our family after the service, voluntarily given without a single word from us, was gratefully received. Smile, if you will, about our traditions, but somehow the too-often unheralded women in this Church are *always* there when hands hang down and knees are feeble.[1] They seem to grasp instinctively the divinity in Christ's declaration: "Inasmuch as ye have done it unto one of the least of these . . . , ye have done it unto me."[2]

And no less the brethren of the priesthood. I think, for example, of the leaders of our young men who, depending on the climate and continent, either take bone-rattling fifty-mile hikes or dig—and actually try to sleep in—ice caves for what have to be the longest nights of human experience. I am grateful for memories of my own high priests group, which a few years ago took turns for weeks sleeping on a small recliner in the bedroom of a dying quorum member so that his aged and equally fragile wife could get some sleep through those final weeks of her sweetheart's life. I am grateful for the Church's army of teachers, officers, advisers, and clerks, to say nothing of people who are forever setting up tables and taking down chairs. I am grateful for ordained patriarchs, musicians, family historians, and osteoporotic couples who trundle off to the temple at five o'clock in the morning with little suitcases now almost bigger than they are. I am grateful for selfless parents who—perhaps for a lifetime—care for a challenged child, sometimes with more than one challenge and sometimes with more than one child. I am grateful for children who close ranks later in life to give back to ill or aging parents.

And to the near-perfect elderly sister who almost apologetically whispered recently, "I have never been a leader of anything in the Church. I guess I've only been a helper," I say, "Dear sister, God bless you and all the 'helpers' in the kingdom." Some of us who *are* leaders hope someday to have the standing before God that you have already attained.

Too often I have failed to express gratitude for the faith and goodness of such people in my life. President James E. Faust said some years ago, "As a small boy . . . , I remember my grandmother . . . cooking our delicious meals on a hot wood-stove. When the wood box next to the stove became empty, Grandmother would silently . . . go out to refill it from the pile of cedar wood outside, and bring the heavily laden box back into the house. I was so insensitive . . . [that] I sat there and let my beloved grandmother refill [that] box." Then, his voice choking with emotion, he said, "I feel ashamed of myself and have regretted my omission for all of my life. I hope someday to ask for her forgiveness."[3]

If a man as perfect as I felt President Faust was can acknowledge his youthful oversight, I can do no less than make a similar admission and pay a long-overdue tribute of my own.

When I was called to serve a mission back before the dawn of time, there was no equalization of missionary costs. Each had to bear the full expense of the mission to which he or she was sent. Some missions were very expensive, and, as it turned out, mine was one of those.

As we encourage missionaries to do, I had saved money and sold personal belongings to pay my own way as best I could. I *thought* I had enough money, but I wasn't sure how it would be in the final months of my mission. With that question on my mind, I nevertheless blissfully left my family for the greatest experience anyone could hope to have. I loved my mission as I am sure no young man has ever loved one before or since.

Then I returned home just as my parents were called to serve a mission of their own. What would I do now? How in the world could I pay for a college education? How could I possibly pay for board and room? And how could I realize the great dream of my heart, to marry the breathtakingly perfect Patricia Terry? I don't mind admitting that I was discouraged and frightened.

Hesitantly I went to the local bank and asked the manager, a family friend, how much was in my account. He looked surprised and said, "Why, Jeff, it's *all* in your account. Didn't they tell you? Your parents wanted to do what little they could to help you get started when you got home. They didn't withdraw a cent during your mission. I supposed that you knew."

Well, I didn't know. What I do know is that my dad, a self-educated accountant, a "bookkeeper" as they were called in our little town, with very few clients, probably never wore a new suit or a new shirt or a new pair of shoes for two years so his son could have all of those for his mission. Furthermore, what I did not know but then came to know was that my mother, who had never worked out of the home in her married life, took a job at a local department store so that my mission expenses could be met. And not one word of that was ever conveyed to me on my mission. Not a single word was said regarding any of it. How many fathers in this Church have done exactly what my father did? And how many mothers, in these difficult economic times, are still doing what my mother did?

To you, Mom and Dad, and to all the moms and dads and families and faithful people everywhere, I thank you for sacrificing for your children (and for other people's children!), for wanting so much to give them advantages you never had, for wanting so much to give them the happiest life you could provide.

My thanks to all you wonderful members of the Church—and legions of good people not of our faith—for proving every day of your life that the pure love of Christ "never faileth."[4] No one of you is insignificant, in part because you make the gospel of Jesus Christ what it is—a living reminder of His grace and mercy, a private but powerful manifestation in small villages and large cities of the good He did and the life He gave bringing peace and salvation to other people. We are honored beyond expression to be counted one with you in such a sacred cause.

Brothers and sisters, seeing your example, I pledge anew *my* determination to be better, to be more faithful—more kind and devoted, more charitable and true as our Father in Heaven is and as so many of you already are. As Jesus said to the Nephites, so say I: "Because of your faith . . . , my joy is full. And when he had said these words, he wept."[5]

NOTES

From a talk given at general conference, October 2010.

1. See Hebrews 12:12; Doctrine and Covenants 81:5.
2. Matthew 25:40.
3. James E. Faust, "The Weightier Matters of the Law: Judgment, Mercy, and Faith," *Ensign*, November 1997, 59.
4. 1 Corinthians 13:8; see also Moroni 7:46–47.
5. 3 Nephi 17:20–21.

NOT ALL
ANGELS

are from the other side of the veil.

SOME OF THEM

we walk with and talk with—

HERE, NOW, EVERY DAY.

To my friends who are
instruments in the hands of God

CHAPTER 15

THE MINISTRY OF ANGELS

When Adam and Eve willingly stepped into mortality, they knew this telestial world would contain thorns and thistles and troubles of every kind. Perhaps their most challenging realization, however, was not the hardship and danger they would endure but the fact that they would now be distanced from God, separated from Him with whom they had walked and talked, who had given them face-to-face counsel. After this conscious choice, as the record of creation says, "they saw him not; for they were shut out from his presence."[1] Amidst all else that must have troubled them, surely this must have troubled them the most.

But God knew the challenges they would face, and He

certainly knew how lonely and troubled they would sometimes feel. So He watched over His mortal family constantly, heard their prayers always, and sent prophets (and later apostles) to teach, counsel, and guide them. But in times of special need, He sent angels, divine messengers, to bless His children, to re-assure them that heaven was always very close and that His help was always very near. Indeed, shortly after Adam and Eve found themselves in the lone and dreary world, an angel appeared unto them,[2] who taught them the meaning of their sacrifice and the atoning role of the promised Redeemer who was to come.

When the time for this Savior's advent was at hand, an angel was sent to announce to Mary that she was to be the mother of the Son of God.[3] Then a host of angels was commissioned to sing on the night the baby Jesus was born.[4] Shortly thereafter an angel would announce to Joseph that the new-born baby was in danger and that this little family must flee to Egypt for safety.[5] When it was safe to return, an angel conveyed that information to the family and the three returned to the land of their heritage.[6]

From the beginning down through the dispensations, God has used angels as His emissaries in conveying love and concern for His children. The scriptures and our own latter-day history are filled with accounts of angels ministering to those on earth—rich doctrine and rich history indeed.

Usually such beings are *not* seen. Sometimes they are. But seen or unseen, they are *always* near. Sometimes their assignments are very grand and have significance for the whole world. Sometimes the messages are more private. Occasionally the angelic purpose is to warn. But most often it is to comfort, to provide some form of merciful attention, guidance in difficult times. When in Lehi's dream he found himself in a frightening place, "a dark and dreary waste," as he described it, he was met by an angel, "a man . . . dressed in a white robe; . . . he spake unto me," Lehi said, "and bade me follow him."[7] Lehi did follow him to safety and ultimately to the path of salvation.

In the course of life all of us spend time in "dark and dreary" places, wildernesses, circumstances of sorrow or fear or discouragement. Our present day is filled with global distress over financial crises, energy problems, terrorist attacks, and natural calamities. These translate into individual and family concerns not only about homes in which to live and food available to eat but also about the ultimate safety and well-being of our children and the latter-day prophecies about our planet. More serious than these—and sometimes related to them—are matters of ethical, moral, and spiritual decay seen in populations large and small, at home and abroad. But I testify that angels are *still* sent to help *us,* even as they were sent to help Adam and Eve, to help the prophets, and indeed to help the Savior of the world Himself. Matthew records in his gospel that after Satan had tempted Christ in the wilderness, "angels came and ministered unto him."[8] Even the Son of God, a God Himself, had need for heavenly comfort during His sojourn in mortality. And so such ministrations will be to the righteous until the end of time. As Mormon said to his son Moroni, who would one day *be* an angel:

"Has the day of miracles ceased?

"Or have angels ceased to appear unto the children of men? Or has he withheld the power of the Holy Ghost from them? Or will he, so long as time shall last, or the earth shall stand, or there shall be one man upon the face thereof to be saved?

"Behold I say unto you, Nay; for . . . it is by faith that angels appear and minister unto men, . . .

"For behold, they are subject unto [Christ], to minister according to the word of his command, showing themselves unto them of strong faith and a firm mind in every form of godliness."[9]

I ask you to take heart, be filled with faith, and remember the Lord has said He "would fight [*our*] battles, [our] children's battles, and [the battles of our] children's children."[10] And what do we do to merit such a defense? We are to "search diligently, pray always, and be believing[. Then] all things shall work together for [our] good, if [we] walk uprightly and remember the covenant wherewith [we] have covenanted."[11] The latter days are *not* a time to fear and tremble. They *are* a time to be believing and remember our covenants.

I have spoken here of heavenly help, of angels dispatched to bless us in time of need. But when we speak of those who are instruments in the hand of God, we are reminded that not all angels are from the other side of the veil. Some of them we walk with and talk with—here, now, every day. Some of them reside in our own neighborhoods. Some of them gave birth to us, and in my case, one of them consented to marry me. Indeed heaven never seems closer than when we see the love of God manifested in the kindness and devotion of people so good and so pure that *angelic* is the only word that comes to mind.

I want to share with you an account by my friend and BYU colleague, the late Clyn D. Barrus. I do so with the permission of his wife, Marilyn, and their family.

Referring to his childhood on a large Idaho farm, Brother Barrus spoke of his nightly assignment to round up the cows at milking time. Because the cows pastured in a field bordered by the occasionally treacherous Teton River, the strict rule in the Barrus household was that during the spring flood season the children were *never* to go after any cows who ventured across the river. They were always to return home and seek mature help.

One Saturday just after his seventh birthday, Brother Barrus's parents promised the family a night at the movies if the chores were done on time. But when young Clyn arrived at the pasture, the cows he sought had crossed the river, even though it was running at high flood stage. Knowing his rare night at the movies was in jeopardy, he decided to go after the cows himself, even though he had been warned many times never to do so.

As the seven-year-old urged his old horse, Banner, down

into the cold, swift stream, the horse's head barely cleared the water. An adult sitting on the horse would have been safe, but at Brother Barrus's tender age, the current completely covered him except when the horse lunged forward several times, bringing Clyn's head above water just enough to gasp for air.

Here I turn to Brother Barrus's own words:

"When Banner finally climbed the other bank, I realized that my life had been in grave danger and that I had done a terrible thing—I had knowingly disobeyed my father. I felt that I could redeem myself only by bringing the cows home safely. Maybe then my father would forgive me. But it was already dusk, and I didn't know for sure where I was. Despair overwhelmed me. I was wet and cold, lost and afraid.

"I climbed down from old Banner, fell to the ground by his feet, and began to cry. Between thick sobs, I tried to offer a prayer, repeating over and over to my Father in Heaven, 'I'm sorry. Forgive me! I'm sorry. Forgive me!'

"I prayed for a long time. When I finally looked up, I saw through my tears a figure dressed in white walking toward me. In the dark, I felt certain it must be an angel sent in answer to my prayers. I did not move or make a sound as the figure approached, so overwhelmed was I by what I saw. Would the Lord really send an angel to me, who had been so disobedient?

"Then a familiar voice said, 'Son, I've been looking for you.' In the darkness I recognized the voice of my father and ran to his outstretched arms. He held me tightly, then said gently, 'I was worried. I'm glad I found you.'

"I tried to tell him how sorry I was, but only disjointed words came out of my trembling lips—'Thank you . . . darkness . . . afraid . . . river . . . alone.' Later that night I learned that when I had not returned from the pasture, my father had come looking for me. When neither I nor the cows were to be found, he knew I had crossed the river and was in danger. Because it was dark and time was of the essence, he removed his clothes down to his long white thermal underwear, tied his shoes around his neck, and swam a treacherous river to rescue a wayward son."[12]

My beloved brothers and sisters, I testify of angels, both the heavenly and the mortal kind. In doing so I am testifying that God never leaves us alone, never leaves us unaided in the challenges that we face. "Nor will he, so long as time shall last, or the earth shall stand, or there shall be one man [or woman or child] upon the face thereof to be saved."[13] On occasions, global or personal, we may feel we are distanced from God, shut out from heaven, lost, alone in dark and dreary places. Often enough that distress can be of our own making, but even then the Father of us all is watching and assisting. And always there are those angels who come and go all around us, seen and unseen, known and unknown, mortal and immortal.

May we all believe more readily in, and have more gratitude for, the Lord's promise as contained in one of President Thomas S. Monson's favorite scriptures: "I will go before your face. I will be on your right hand and on your left, . . . my Spirit shall be in your [heart], and mine angels round about you, to bear you up."[14] In the process of praying for those angels to attend us, may we all try to be a little more angelic ourselves—with a kind word, a strong arm, a declaration of faith and "the covenant wherewith [we] have covenanted."[15] Perhaps then *we* can be emissaries sent from God when someone is crying, "Darkness . . . afraid . . . river . . . alone."

NOTES

From a talk given at general conference, October 2008.

1. Moses 5:4.
2. See Moses 5:6–8.
3. See Luke 1:26–38.
4. See Luke 2:8–14.
5. See Matthew 2:13–15.
6. See Matthew 2:19–23.
7. 1 Nephi 8: 7, 5–6.
8. Matthew 4:11.
9. Moroni 7:35–37, 30.
10. Doctrine and Covenants 98:37.
11. Doctrine and Covenants 90:24.
12. See Clyn D. Barrus, "Coming Home," *Friend,* April 1995, 2–4.
13. Moroni 7:36.
14. Doctrine and Covenants 84:88.
15. Doctrine and Covenants 90:24.

GOD KNOWS WHAT YOU NEED.

He wants you to *pray* about

what you need, and He wants you

to *work* for it. But mostly

He wants you to *believe*

HE CAN AND WILL PROVIDE.

To my friends
who stand as witnesses

⎯⎯⎯ ∾ ⎯⎯⎯

CHAPTER 16

MOVE FORWARD WITH FAITH

We live in troubled times. You read the newspaper. You watch the evening news. You catch something on the Internet. However you get your news or whatever talk you have with your friends and family members, you're aware that we have a lot of problems in the world.

Those problems include the reality of war. Places like Afghanistan and Iraq and Iran have come into our everyday conversations. At one time we hardly even knew where they were on the map, and now we think about them every day. Perhaps the problem is the potential for a nuclear holocaust or harm to the environment or avian flu or some other worldwide catastrophe. Other problems can be a lot closer to home.

There's a lot to worry about in life. But it's always been that way. Don't think you've been singled out for some particular burden at a uniquely troublesome time in the history of the world. It's always been a troubling time in the history of the world. This is a fallen world. This is not the celestial kingdom; this is the telestial kingdom. It's mortal, and it's filled with thorns and thistles and noxious weeds at local, national, and international levels, at home and abroad, in private and in public.

That is the way it always will be until the Lord comes. We apparently understood that when we agreed to come here. In fact, the scriptures say we shouted for joy at the prospect of coming. Some days we wonder what all the shouting was about. But we saw it better then, and we'll see it better later. Right now we grope a little in the second act of a play with a first act we're not allowed to remember except in broad brush strokes and a third act we've yet to see in any detail.

So join hands and be filled with faith and enjoy life to the fullest. Embrace the promises and possibilities of this stage of life and this moment in history. C. S. Lewis, who was among the most famous converts to Christianity in the twentieth century, once said, "We are mistaken when we compare our [present situation] to 'normal life.' Life has never been normal. Even those periods we think most tranquil . . . turn out, on closer inspection, to be full of crises, alarms, difficulties, emergencies."[1]

Don't worry about what lies ahead. Live your life and have

faith. Faith begins with faith in the Lord Jesus Christ, and that leads to faith in everything else: faith in the future and faith in our families and faith in our prospects and our promises and our possibilities.

I'm convinced that faith was designated as the first principle of the gospel because somehow our Father in Heaven knew that fear would always be with us. We have to start with faith, because fear, if we let it, can be at every turn. Please don't yield to fear. Fear comes of ignoring what we know. When you truly understand why faith is the first principle of the gospel, you will embrace your faith, live your faith, and declare it to those who are faltering, who are giving in to fear.

It may help to remember that the quote I just shared from C. S. Lewis was given as bombs were dropping on London in the middle of World War II. People were saying then, as they do today, "Why should I go to school? Why should I get married? Why should we have children? Why should I plan anything? I'm going to walk out of here and a bomb will probably drop on me." Well, maybe it will. But it might have happened yesterday, and it could happen tomorrow. Nothing's any different for anybody anytime.

It's just that when bombs are dropping, we tend to think a little more seriously, and that's good. We ought to be a little more serious some of the time, and a bomb tends to get your attention. But don't be a suicide bomber. Don't bring on the very thing you fear. Keep moving, keep believing, keep growing, keep trying. Don't give up, and don't give in. Don't worry so much.

Edward Everett Hale is famous in part because he was the other speaker at Gettysburg when Abraham Lincoln gave his legendary address. How would you like to have been the other speaker at the Gettysburg memorial? Lincoln spoke for a total of four minutes by the clock. Edward Everett Hale spoke for two and a half hours. Although I've never loved Edward Everett Hale's performance, I've loved this one line from him: "Never bear more than one kind of trouble at a time."

I know some people who bear three kinds of trouble at once—all they have had, all they now have, and all they expect to have in the future. But life will be better if you discipline yourself to never bear more than one kind of trouble at a time.

In the New Testament, the Savior is recorded as saying:

"Take no thought, saying, What shall we eat? or, What shall we drink? or, Wherewithal shall we be clothed?

"(For after all these things do the Gentiles seek:) for your heavenly Father knoweth that ye have need of all these things.

"But seek ye first the kingdom of God, and his righteousness; and all these things shall be added unto you.

"Take therefore no thought for the morrow: for the morrow shall take thought for the things of itself. Sufficient unto the day is the evil thereof."[2]

In Third Nephi, some of the words in that last sentence are reversed. The change adds an interesting slant of light on that phrase. The Book of Mormon says, "Sufficient is the day unto the evil thereof,"[3] as opposed to "sufficient unto the day is the evil thereof." At one point the emphasis is on the day; on the other, the emphasis is on the troubles you can have in the day. In either case, the Lord is counseling us to seek first the kingdom of God and not worry overly much about tomorrow.

Now, technically and officially, those words were spoken to the Twelve who followed Jesus, and I suppose they have very special application to my Brethren and me. We really aren't supposed to worry about anything of a personal, temporal nature, any kind of food or clothing or housing or whatever. We just go wherever we are sent on the Lord's work, and we come back when we are told to come back. But the principle of that divine counsel still applies to you.

Yes, you have to do some planning. You have to be realistic about making some progress, about preparing for the future. But we take too much heed about things that need not worry us—what we will eat, what we will drink, how we will be clothed. Take no thought, or at least less thought, for those things, as measured against thinking of the kingdom of God and His righteousness.

"All these things shall be added unto you." That's the part of the scripture almost nobody remembers. We always quote "Seek first the kingdom of God." We always quote "Take no thought for the morrow." But we frequently forget that the Savior said "All these things shall be added unto you."

God knows what you need. He wants you to pray about what you need, and He wants you to work for it. But mostly

He wants you to believe He can and will provide. Seek the kingdom of God and His righteousness and remember that the troubles of this day are enough. Don't worry about yesterday, and don't worry about tomorrow. Don't be one of those Edward Everett Hale victims who worry about all the troubles they can think of that have ever existed or ever will exist.

We live in a very acquisitive society. (Maybe societies have always been acquisitive.) The prevailing concern seems to be, "What can I get; what's in it for me?" And some things are supposed to be for you. But while you're getting, remember to give. Remember that there are others who are striving and others who have needs. I'm not talking now just about financial needs. These needs can be emotional and social. And to meet such needs, you may be called upon to extend courtesies and kindnesses, perhaps even sacrifice some of your own financial or emotional resources.

That's the general rule: find a way to give, find a way to sacrifice. You'll do better and be better and feel better if you've extended your hand and your offering. Maybe all you have to give is your love, your kindness. Maybe it's just time and courtesy. But sometimes, that's the most important thing to give.

Another important thing for you to share is your witness of the truth. I fell in love with this passage from theologian George MacDonald more than thirty years ago:

"Is every Christian expected to bear witness? A man content to bear no witness to the truth is not in the kingdom of heaven. One who believes must bear witness. One who sees the truth, must live witnessing to it. Is our life, then, a witnessing to the truth? Do we carry ourselves in bank, on farm, in house or shop, in study or chamber or workshop, as the Lord would, or as the Lord would not? Are we careful to be true? . . . When contempt is cast on the truth, do we smile? Wronged in our presence, do we make no sign that we hold by it? I do not say we are called upon to dispute, and defend with logic and argument, but we are called upon to show that we are on the other side. . . . The soul that loves the truth and tries to be true will know when to speak and when to be silent; but the true man [or woman] will never look as if he did not care. We are not bound to say all we think, but we are bound not even to look what we do not think."[4]

Is every Christian expected to bear witness? There's a lot more message here than simply saying "every member a missionary," though we believe that, too. I'm talking about who you are, who you're determined to be, who you are down to the marrow of your bones. I'm talking about the devotion and determination and loyalty to gospel truth that you always let shine through your words and actions.

Essentially this same call came at the waters of Mormon. Alma said there:

"As ye are desirous to come into the fold of God, and to be called his people, and are willing to bear one another's burdens, that they may be light;

"Yea, and are willing to mourn with those that mourn; yea, and comfort those that stand in need of comfort, and to stand as witnesses of God at all times and in all things, and in all places that ye may be in, even until death, . . .

"Now I say unto you, if this be the desire of your hearts, what have you against being baptized in the name of the Lord, as a witness before him that ye have entered into a covenant with him . . . ?"[5]

What does it mean to be a witness at all times and in all places and in all circumstances that you are in? It applies in all situations, not just missionary circumstances. Yet I feel particular pain when I meet returned missionaries who don't understand what their missions were supposed to mean to them for the rest of their lives.

I've said all over this Church that my mission meant everything to me. I believe no young man ever went on a mission and had it affect him more than my mission affected me. This much I know: my mission has affected every conscious decision and aspect of my later life since those nineteenth through twenty-first years of my earlier life.

No one in my immediate family had ever been on a mission. I was pioneering. I didn't even know what to take for clothing. And I didn't know what to do when I got there. I didn't have anybody to consult with about it, but it turned out to be the grandest, most formative, most powerful experience of my young life. It has shaped and touched and affected everything that I've ever done since and every blessing I've had—my marriage to Sister Holland, our children, what we've taught our children, what we want them yet to be, their missions, and now their temple marriages and their children, professional decisions and opportunities, Church experience. All of those wonderful things have come to me because I served a faithful mission.

That's one of the reasons I get nervous—in fact, I get more than nervous, I get exercised—if I think that a missionary has been out in the field and has come home thinking, "Well, I got those two years out of the way [or if it's a sister, those eighteen months]. I've done my bit, and now it's back to real life."

No sir! *That* was real life: the mission, the gospel, the truth—that's real life! Don't ever go downhill from that. We do actually let you take your name plaque off. But we don't want anybody saying, "Well, that was life of another order, and now I'm going to just settle back and be a regular fellow." No sir! Not here. Not now. Not in this Church! We keep moving and we keep climbing and we keep trying and we keep believing.

If you could be a witness out there, why can't you be a witness here? A witness is a witness. A believer is a believer. A testimony is forever. If the gospel was true in Santiago, or Montevideo, or Johannesburg, or Jakarta, or Tokyo, or Tallahassee . . . if it was true there, it's true here. Live it and believe it and stand for it forever. Stand in front of my children and my grandchildren and tell them what your belief is now and what your life is like now. Don't disappoint them. Is what you were witnessing then what you are witnessing now? You hold those deacons spellbound. Impress those Mia Maids.

I believe in people who bear witness. I believe in the call

to testify, a call that lasts a lifetime. I'm not saying you have to keep giving lessons. I'm not saying you have to go knock on doors. You can if you want to, and I do hope you'll help the missionaries. I hope you take advantage of every opportunity to testify. But I'm not talking so much about knocking on doors as I am about simply being a living witness "at all times and in all things, and in all places."

I pray that you will live this gospel, that you will love it, that it will mean something to you. And if you're a new convert, then so much the better; it means that much more to you now. Brigham Young said, "Be righteous in the dark."[6] I want you to be righteous in the dark and in the morning and in the afternoon, and yesterday and tomorrow. I want you to be filled with integrity in terms of moral issues, in terms of resisting pornography, in terms of faithful devotion in the kingdom of God. I want you to be honorable in the community and honorable in your professions, whatever they are or are going to be.

I don't have the capacity to develop all of the ways you can bear witness, all the ways you can be a man or woman of Christ. I'm just asking you to stand firm and faithful, to pour concrete right down the center of your spine. Square your shoulders and face the world and say, "I don't know who's on my left, and I don't know who's on my right, but I know I am here! Count me in!"

I have thought so many times in my life of the power of a single individual, or a couple of individuals who team up together and face the future and fight the good fight. We don't have to rehearse the lives of apostles and prophets, missionaries and great leaders; the world is filled with great people—with people just like you. You may be thinking, "I'm not much and don't add up to much, and who am I to be compared with great men and women? I'm only one person, and I've got problems." But somehow it's been people like you who have changed the course of human history.

It has been people like you who have said they weren't going to yield to history; they were going to make it. They weren't going to be subdued by history; they were going to shape it. So you just grab life by the lapels and use the strength that God has given you in this, the true and living Church of the true and living God.

We are not going to be like Peter and be crucified upside down. We are not going to be like Paul and be beheaded and drawn and quartered and have our body parts taken to all four corners of the city of Rome. That is not likely to happen in our generation.

No, the question in our time is *not* "Is this dispensation going to endure?" because we know that answer. Yes, it will endure and triumph. The question is, will it endure and triumph with you, or will it have to endure and triumph without you? Please stay true and embrace these blessings forever. In this great, grand contest we *know* who wins, and yet too many of us are still trying to decide which team we're going to play for.

I testify that the victory is already recorded. Jesus is the Christ. He is the Savior and the Redeemer of the world. This is the true and living Church. Those are facts. It doesn't matter whether you or I agree or don't agree—that is simply the truth. And now we're called to align our lives with those great, grand principles of this dispensation: the light and the truth, the power and the priesthood, the faith and the future that we all have.

Be true and faithful. Live your religion. Stand straight and be firm—and if there's a little wind blowing, just put your face into the wind and go forward. And when you can't go forward, just stand. Just plant your feet and stand immovable for a while if that's all you can do. Be faithful and be true and love the Lord, because He loves you.

My brothers and sisters, I've borne witness all of my life. I testify that as long as I live, that as long as there is breath on my lips and the ability to move my tongue, you will hear me declare that Jesus is the Christ, the Son of the living God, the Savior and Redeemer of the world and the foundation stone of this Church. I testify of that as a witness, commissioned to do so.

I testify that this restored gospel is the truth. Our day is what all the prophets, priests, and kings have sung of, prayed for, and prophesied about since the beginning of time. This is the hour. God bless you for your faithfulness, and may He keep you safe always.

NOTES

From a talk given September 23, 2007, at the Salt Lake Institute of Religion.

1. C. S. Lewis, "Learning in Wartime," in *The Weight of Glory* (2009).
2. Matthew 6:34.
3. 3 Nephi 13:34.
4. George MacDonald, *Unspoken Sermons, Series I, II, and III* (2012), 262.
5. Mosiah 18:8–10.
6. Brigham Young's Office Journal, January 28, 1857, in Church History Library.

Believe in MIRACLES.

I have seen so many of them come

when every other indication would

say that hope was lost.

*To my friends
who suffer*

—————

CHAPTER 17

LIKE A BROKEN VESSEL

The Apostle Peter wrote that disciples of Jesus Christ are to have "compassion one of another."[1] In that spirit I wish to speak to those who suffer from some form of mental illness or emotional disorder, whether those afflictions be slight or severe, of brief duration or persistent over a lifetime. We sense the complexity of such matters when we hear professionals speak of neuroses and psychoses, of genetic predispositions and chromosome defects, of bipolarity, paranoia, and schizophrenia. However bewildering this all may be, these afflictions are some of the realities of mortal life, and there should be no more shame in acknowledging them than in acknowledging a battle with high blood pressure or the sudden appearance of a malignant tumor.

In striving for some peace and understanding in these difficult matters, it is crucial to remember that we are living—and chose to live—in a fallen world where for divine purposes our pursuit of godliness will be tested and tried again and again. Of greatest assurance in God's plan is that a Savior was promised, a Redeemer, who through our faith in Him would lift us triumphantly over those tests and trials, even though the cost to do so would be unfathomable for both the Father who sent Him and the Son who came. It is only an appreciation of this divine love that will make our own lesser suffering first bearable, then understandable, and finally redemptive.

Let me leave the extraordinary illnesses I have mentioned to concentrate on MDD—"major depressive disorder"—or, more commonly, "depression." When I speak of this, I am not speaking of bad hair days, tax deadlines, or other discouraging moments we all have. Everyone is going to be anxious or downhearted on occasion. The Book of Mormon says Ammon and his brethren were depressed at a very difficult time,[2] and so can the rest of us be. But today I am speaking of something more serious, of an affliction so severe that it significantly restricts a person's ability to function fully, a crater in the mind so deep that no one can responsibly suggest it would surely go away if those victims would just square their shoulders and think more positively—though I am a vigorous advocate of square shoulders and positive thinking!

No, this dark night of the mind and spirit is more than mere discouragement. I have seen it come to an absolutely angelic man when his beloved spouse of fifty years passed away. I have seen it in new mothers with what is euphemistically labeled "after-baby blues." I have seen it strike anxious students, military veterans, and grandmothers worried about the well-being of their grown children.

And I have seen it in young fathers trying to provide for their families. In that regard I once terrifyingly saw it in myself. At one point in our married life when financial fears collided with staggering fatigue, I took a psychic blow that was as unanticipated as it was real. With the grace of God and the love of my family, I kept functioning and kept working, but even after all these years I continue to feel a deep sympathy for others more chronically or more deeply afflicted with such gloom than I was. In any case we have all taken courage from those who, in the words of the Prophet Joseph, "search[ed] . . . and contemplate[d] the darkest abyss"[3] and persevered through it—not the least of whom were Abraham Lincoln, Winston Churchill, and Elder George Albert Smith, the latter being one of the most gentle and Christlike men of our dispensation, who battled recurring depression for some years before later becoming the universally beloved eighth prophet and President of The Church of Jesus Christ of Latter-day Saints.

So how do you best respond when mental or emotional challenges confront you or those you love? Above all, never lose faith in your Father in Heaven, who loves you more than you can comprehend. As President Thomas S. Monson has said: "That love never changes. . . . It is there for you when you are sad or happy, discouraged or hopeful. God's love is there for you whether or not you feel you deserve [it]. It is simply always there."[4] Never, ever doubt that, and never harden your heart. Faithfully pursue the time-tested devotional practices that bring the Spirit of the Lord into your life. Seek the counsel of those who hold keys for your spiritual well-being. Ask for and cherish priesthood blessings. Take the sacrament every week, and hold fast to the perfecting promises of the Atonement of Jesus Christ. Believe in miracles. I have seen so many of them come when every other indication would say that hope was lost. Hope is *never* lost. If those miracles do not come soon or fully or seemingly at all, remember the Savior's own anguished example: if the bitter cup does not pass, drink it and be strong, trusting in happier days ahead.[5]

In preventing illness whenever possible, watch for the stress indicators in yourself and in others you may be able to help. As with your automobile, be alert to rising temperatures, excessive speed, or a tank low on fuel. When you face "depletion depression," make the requisite adjustments. Fatigue is the common enemy of us all—so slow down, rest up, replenish, and refill. Physicians promise us that if we do not take time to be well, we most assuredly will take time later on to be ill.

If things continue to be debilitating, seek the advice of reputable people with certified training, professional skills, and good values. Be honest with them about your history and your struggles. Prayerfully and responsibly consider the counsel they give and the solutions they prescribe. If you had appendicitis,

God would expect you to seek a priesthood blessing *and* get the best medical care available. So too with emotional disorders. Our Father in Heaven expects us to use *all* of the marvelous gifts He has provided in this glorious dispensation.

If you are the one afflicted or a caregiver to such, try not to be overwhelmed with the size of your task. Don't assume you can fix everything, but fix what you can. If those are only small victories, be grateful for them and be patient. Dozens of times in the scriptures, the Lord commands someone to "stand still" or "be still"—and wait.[6] Patiently enduring some things is part of our mortal education.

For caregivers, in your devoted effort to assist with another's health, do not destroy your own. In all these things be wise. Do not run faster than you have strength.[7] Whatever else you may or may not be able to provide, you can offer your prayers and you can give "love unfeigned."[8] "Charity suffereth long, and is kind; . . . [it] beareth all things, . . . hopeth all things, endureth all things. Charity *never* faileth."[9]

Also let us remember that through any illness or difficult challenge, there is still much in life to be hopeful about and grateful for. We are infinitely more than our limitations or our afflictions! Stephanie Clark Nielson and her family have been our friends for more than thirty years. On August 16, 2008, Stephanie and her husband, Christian, were in a plane crash and subsequent fire that scarred her so horrifically that only her painted toenails were recognizable when family members came to identify the victims. There was almost no chance Stephanie could live. After three months in a sleep-induced coma, she awoke to see herself. With that, the psyche-scarring and horrendous depression came. Having four children under the age of seven, Stephanie did not want them to see her ever again. She felt it would be better not to live. "I thought it would be easier," Stephanie once told me in my office, "if they just forgot about me and I quietly slipped out of their life."

But to her eternal credit, and with the prayers of her husband, family, friends, four beautiful children, and a fifth born to the Nielsons after the accident, Stephanie fought her way back from the abyss of self-destruction to be one of the most popular "mommy bloggers" in the nation, openly declaring to the four million who follow her blog that her "divine purpose" in life is to be a mom and to cherish *every day* she has been given on this beautiful earth.

Whatever your struggle—mental or emotional or physical or otherwise—do not vote against the preciousness of life by ending it! Trust in God. Hold on in His love. Know that one day the dawn will break brightly and all shadows of mortality will flee. Though we may feel we are "like a broken vessel," as the Psalmist says,[10] we must remember, that vessel is in the hands of the divine potter. Broken minds can be healed just the way broken bones and broken hearts are healed. While God is at work making those repairs, the rest of us can help by being merciful, nonjudgmental, and kind.

I testify of the holy Resurrection, that unspeakable cornerstone gift in the Atonement of the Lord Jesus Christ! With the

Apostle Paul, I testify that that which was sown in corruption will one day be raised in incorruption and that which was sown in weakness will ultimately be raised in power.[11] I bear witness of that day when loved ones whom we knew to have disabilities in mortality will stand before us glorified and grand, breathtakingly perfect in body and mind. What a thrilling moment that will be! I do not know whether we will be happier for ourselves that we have witnessed such a miracle or happier for them that they are fully perfect and finally "free at last."[12] Until that hour when Christ's consummate gift is evident to us all, may we live by faith, hold fast to hope, and show "compassion one of another."[13]

NOTES

From a talk given at general conference, October 2013.

1. 1 Peter 3:8.
2. See Alma 26:27; see also Alma 56:16.
3. *Teachings of Presidents of the Church: Joseph Smith* (2007), 267.
4. Thomas S. Monson, "We Never Walk Alone," *Ensign,* November 2013, 123, 124.
5. See Matthew 26:39.
6. See, for example, Psalm 4:4; Doctrine and Covenants 101:16.
7. See Mosiah 4:27.
8. Doctrine and Covenants 121:41.
9. 1 Corinthians 13:4, 7–8; emphasis added; see also Moroni 7:45–46.
10. Psalm 31:12.
11. See 1 Corinthians 15:42–43.
12. "Free at Last," in John W. Work, comp., *American Negro Songs: 230 Folk Songs and Spirituals, Religious and Secular* (1998), 197.
13. 1 Peter 3:8.

HAPPINESS

comes first by what

comes into your head

a long time before

material blessings come

into your hand.

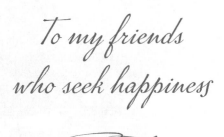

To my friends
who seek happiness

CHAPTER 18

LIVING AFTER THE MANNER OF HAPPINESS

In a phrase I am sure you have heard many times, generally attributed to the Prophet Joseph Smith, he said that "Happiness is the object and design of our existence; and will be the end thereof, if we pursue the path that leads to it."[1]

It is that worthy quest for happiness that I wish to address. Note that I said "quest for happiness," not happiness itself. Remember the Prophet Joseph's choice of language: He spoke of *the path that leads to happiness* as the key to realizing that goal.

By the way, this is not a new quest; it has been one of the fundamental pursuits of humankind down through the ages of time. One of the greatest intellectual minds the Western world has ever known once said, "Happiness is the meaning and purpose of life, the whole aim and end of human existence."[2] That was Aristotle, but note how presciently his statement parallels that of the Prophet Joseph—almost the exact phrasing.

In the opening lines of the Declaration of Independence, Thomas Jefferson immortalized both our personal and political quests by forever linking (at least in America) the three great inalienable rights of life, liberty, and the pursuit of happiness. But notice in that magnificent troika it is not *happiness* that is a right (like life and liberty), but specifically the *pursuit* of happiness.

So how do we "pursue" happiness, especially when life lies ahead of us as a challenging mountain to climb? Well, we know one thing for sure: happiness is not easy to find running straight for it. It is usually too elusive, too ephemeral, too subtle. Most times happiness comes to us when we least expect it, when we are busy doing something else. Happiness is almost always a by-product of some other endeavor. One of my favorite writers from my university days, Henry David Thoreau said, "Happiness is like a butterfly; the more you chase it, the more it will elude you, but if you turn your attention to other things, it will come and sit softly on your shoulder."[3] This is one of those great gospel ironies that often don't seem to make sense, like "the last shall be first" and "lose your life to find it."[4] The gospel is filled with such ironies and indirections, and I think the pursuit of happiness is one of them. So how do we optimize our chance for happiness without pursuing it so directly that we miss it? Let me go to a most remarkable book for some answers.

The first thirty years of Book of Mormon history do not present a pleasant story. After the abrupt necessity of abandoning their entire earthly fortune, leaving Jerusalem hastily on the eve of international conflict, crossing the Arabian Peninsula in the most adverse of circumstances, building a boat without any prior experience in doing so, crossing an ocean with would-be fatal conflicts breaking out repeatedly, and landing in a primitive, unknown new land with all the hardship such a settlement would entail, the hostility within the family of Lehi and Sariah became so intense that the two halves of their family split asunder, with one group fleeing yet farther into the wilderness, fearing for their lives lest they fall victim to the bloodthirsty quest of the other. As they plunged into unsettled terrain to seek safety and fashion a life for themselves as best they could, the prophet-leader of this Nephite half of the family says they now tried to live "after the manner of happiness."[5]

In light of what they had just been through for thirty years, and with what we know yet lay in store for them in the trials almost constantly ahead, such a comment seems almost painful. How could any of this be described as anything remotely like "happiness"? There is the rub. Nephi does not say they were happy, though it is evident they actually were. What he says is, they "lived *after the manner of happiness.*" There is a wonderful key in that phrase that can unlock precious blessings for you the rest of your life.

I do not think God in His glory or the angels of heaven or the prophets on earth intend to make us happy all the time, every day in every way, given the testing and trials this earthly realm is intended to provide. As President James E. Faust once phrased it: "Happiness is not given to us in a package that we can just open up and consume. Nobody," he said, "is ever happy 24 hours a day, seven days a week."[6] But my reassurance to you is that in God's plan we can do very much to find the happiness we do desire. We can take certain steps, we can form certain habits, we can do certain things that God and history tell us lead to happiness with the confidence that *if we live in such a manner,* that butterfly is much more likely to land upon our shoulder.

In short, your best chance for being happy is to *do the things that happy people do.* Live the way happy people live. Walk the path that happy people walk. And your chances to find joy in unexpected moments, to find peace in unexpected places, to find the help of angels when you didn't even know they knew you existed, improves exponentially. Here are at least a couple of ideas about how one might live "*after the manner of happiness.*"

Above all else, ultimate happiness, true peace, and anything even remotely close to scriptural joy are found first, foremost, and forever in living the gospel of Jesus Christ. Lots of other philosophies and systems of belief have been tried. Indeed it seems safe to say that virtually *every* other philosophy and system has been tried down through the centuries of history. But when the Apostle Thomas asked the Lord the question people often ask today, "How can we know the way?" Jesus gave the answer that rings from eternity to all eternity, "I am the way, the truth, and the life. . . . And whatsoever ye shall ask in my name, that will I do. . . . If ye shall ask any thing in my name, I will do it."[7]

What a promise! Live my way, live my truth, live my life—live *in this manner* that I am showing you and teaching you—and whatsoever you ask will be given, whatsoever you seek you will find, including happiness. Parts of the blessing may come soon, parts may come later, and parts may not come until heaven, but they will come—all of them. What encouragement that is after a blue Monday or a sad Tuesday or a tearful Wednesday! And it is a promise the realization of which *cannot come any other way* than by devotion to eternal truth! In the words of then newly ordained Elder David O. McKay just short of a full century ago, "[Unlike gratification or pleasure or some kind of thrill, true] happiness is found only along that well beaten [gospel] track, *narrow as it is, . . . [and] straight [as it is],* which leads to life eternal."[8] So love God and each other, and be true to the gospel of Jesus Christ.

Second, learn as quickly as you can that so much of your happiness is in your hands, not in events or circumstances or fortune or misfortune. That is part of what the battle for agency was over in the premortal councils of heaven. We have choice, we have volition, we have agency, and we can choose if not happiness per se then *to live after the manner of it.* Abraham

Lincoln had plenty to be unhappy about in perhaps the most difficult administration a president of the United States has ever faced, but even he reflected that "folks are usually about as happy as they make up their minds to be."[9]

I plead with you not to waste a lot of time or energy or emotion thinking happiness is going to be in how much money you make or what size of house you live in or how attractive you are. On any given day there must be at least ten million testimonials from those who say that nice as some of those things are, they are not the things that bring happiness. Happiness comes first by what comes into your head a long time before material blessings come into your hand. Joseph Smith was living "after the manner of happiness" in a very unhappy situation when he wrote from Liberty Jail to those on the outside who were also the victims of great injustice and persecution: "Let virtue garnish thy thoughts unceasingly; then shall thy confidence wax strong in the presence of God; . . . The Holy Ghost shall be thy constant companion, and thy scepter an unchanging scepter of righteousness and truth."[10]

Let virtue garnish thy thoughts unceasingly. That is not only good counsel against the modern plague of pornography, but it is counsel for all kinds of gospel thoughts, good thoughts, constructive thoughts, hopeful thoughts. Those faith-filled thoughts will alter how you see life's problems and how you find resolution to them. "The Lord requireth the heart and a willing mind,"[11] the revelations say. Too often we have thought it was all up to the heart; it is not. God expects a willing mind in the quest for happiness and peace as well. Put your head into this. And if you do have some negative thoughts from time to time, don't give them expression. When spoken, words take on a life of their own, but thoughts can die quickly if we do not give utterance to them. All of this takes effort. It is a battle, but a battle for happiness that is worth waging. In her popular book *Eat, Pray, Love,* Elizabeth Gilbert wrote: "Happiness is the consequence of personal effort. You fight for it, strive for it, insist upon it, and . . . look for it. You have to participate relentlessly in the manifestations of your own blessings. And once you have achieved a state of happiness, you must never become lax about maintaining it. You must make a mighty effort to keep swimming upward into that happiness . . . , to stay afloat on top of it."[12]

I love that phrase of hers: "Participate relentlessly in the manifestations of your own blessings." Don't be passive. "Keep swimming upward into [your] happiness,"[13] she says. Be determined. Think and speak and act positively. That is what happy people do; that is one aspect of *living after the manner of happiness.*

Here is another. In anticipation of addressing this topic, I sat in my study for a long time trying to think if I had ever known a happy person who was unkind or unpleasant to be with. And guess what? I couldn't think of one—not a single, solitary one. So learn this great truth: You can never, worlds without end, build your happiness on someone else's unhappiness. Sometimes, maybe especially when we are young and insecure and trying to make our way up in the world, we think if we can tear someone else down a little, it will somehow miraculously lift us up. That is what bullying is. That is what catty remarks are. That is what arrogance and superficiality and exclusiveness are. Perhaps we think if we are negative enough, or cynical enough, or just plain mean enough, then expectations won't be too high; we can keep everyone down to a flaw-filled level and therefore our flaws won't be so glaring.

Happy people aren't negative or cynical or mean, so don't plan on that being part of the "manner" of happiness. If my life has taught me anything, it is that kindness and pleasantness and faith-based optimism are characteristics of happy people. From the words of Mother Teresa, "Let no one ever come to you without leaving better and happier. Be the living expression of God's kindness: kindness in your face, kindness in your eyes, kindness in your smile."[14]

A related step along the path toward happiness is to avoid animosity, contention, and anger in your life. Remember it is Lucifer, Satan, the adversary of us all who loves anger. He is "the father of contention, and he stirreth up the hearts of men to contend with anger, one with another."[15] After quoting that verse in general conference a few years ago, Elder Lynn Robbins said, "[That] verb *stir* sounds like a recipe for disaster: Put tempers on medium heat, stir in a few choice words, and bring to a boil; continue stirring until thick; cool off; let feelings chill for several days; serve cold; lots of leftovers."[16] "Lots of leftovers" indeed.

Anger damages or destroys almost everything it touches. As someone has said, to harbor anger is like drinking poison and waiting for the other person to die. It is a vicious acid that will destroy the container long before it does damage to the intended object. There is nothing in it or its cousinly vices—violence, rage, bitterness, and hate—that has anything to do with living the gospel or the pursuit of happiness. I do not think that anger can exist—or at least can be fostered and entertained and indulged in—in a life being lived "after the manner of happiness."

One last suggestion when there are so many others we should consider: that original verse from Nephi said that in an effort to find happiness in their new land after their thirty years of trouble "I, Nephi, did cause my people to be industrious, and to labor with their hands."[17] By contrast, those from whom they fled became "an idle people, full of mischief and subtlety."[18]

If you want to be happy—*work at it*. Learn to work. Serve diligently. Don't be idle and mischievous. A homespun definition of Christlike character might be the integrity to do the right thing at the right time in the right way.

If you will forgive a personal story, let me share with you an educational moment from my own early life. Following my undergraduate years at BYU I taught for two or three years trying to save up enough money for graduate work. I was married and we had our first child, so I knew even with a fellowship it would be pretty tight. During the summers of these teaching years I took courses at local universities, filling in some gaps in my undergraduate education and strengthening my preparation for the graduate field I had chosen.

One summer in Seattle I was taking a class that was particularly demanding. I wasn't exactly ecstatic over the teacher, and the material he used in the course seemed uneven and often unwisely chosen. But I jumped in and tried to ride the waves as best I could.

Just as a major midterm paper was due, my parents called and said they were coming to visit us. That was, of course, wonderful news. They had never been to the Northwest, and we wanted to show them everything. However, time was going to be a bit of a problem. I was teaching a full summer schedule and taking this class on the side. And like the iceberg and the *Titanic* in Thomas Hardy's poem, my parents and this paper descended on me at exactly the same moment. Now, there's no sense even discussing which option was the most attractive to me. We had not seen my parents in more than eighteen months and I've already told you how I felt about this class. Furthermore, it was an optional thing I was doing anyway. After all, this wasn't the university at which I would be doing my graduate work, and certainly no one but I cared whether I did well in it or not.

Well, as fate would have it, my parents arrived on a Friday and my paper was due the next Monday. I had had the good sense to go to work on it reasonably early, so it wasn't as if I had to do it all over one weekend. (I had tried that as an undergraduate and found out it didn't work!) So I had the paper virtually complete, except for one thing. I didn't like it. It wasn't right. I had to work on it some more.

We set everything aside that Friday night and had a great time. My wife made tacos and enchiladas, the art for which my father said he would have banned me from the house if I had not married her. We laughed and talked and had great fun. Then I had a decision to make.

Saturday was a natural day to get up early, drive a couple of hours into British Columbia, meander back down the coast along the Puget Sound, and end up at the Seattle Center to enjoy all the remnants of the World's Fair. That would leave Sunday for my duties as a bishop and then most of Monday to visit some other spots before they left Tuesday to see my brother in California. That posed just one problem. My paper.

Now, I ask you to remember that this was not life and death. I could for all intents and purposes cave in on the course and no one would care. But that didn't seem right to me. So I made a deal with my parents. If they would do all that I outlined with my wife, Pat, and our son, Matt, who was then two, I would stay behind and finish my paper, promising in the process to prepare barbecued steak, tossed green salad, garlic bread, and baked potatoes by the time they got back. With the one proviso, of course, that my dad leave me enough money to find some steak somewhere.

Well, they were a bit disappointed and so was I, but it seemed the best thing to do. So they played and I worked.

I wrote and rewrote and shouted and tore up papers and punched the typewriter and rewrote. (Yes, typewriter. Remember, this was 1967.) It didn't go as smoothly as I had hoped but it went. I finally got it into what seemed reasonably acceptable shape and then threw myself (figuratively, of course) into the tossed salad. Dad had left a dollar or two, Pat had found some steaks at the store, and I had started the coals on the grill with part of the fury I was feeling over paragraphs that wouldn't work. But the paper was finished and the food was on by the time they returned.

Now, that isn't much of a story except that it made a lot of difference in my life. When I got the paper back from the teacher I didn't like much in a course I felt I needed but didn't particularly enjoy, the professor had written just five words. I believe it was the only thing he said to me the whole term. "Publishable paper. See me sometime." Well, the aftermath doesn't really matter except to say that this professor was very close to a faculty member in my intended department at Yale. One thing led to another and he wrote a note saying, in effect, "You may want to consider this chap even if you haven't ever heard of St. George, Utah." There were other contacts along the way and other blessings that came, but my point is that properly completing that paper that summer in that remote setting—remote at least in terms of my ultimate plans—made a lot of difference in my life. To have done otherwise in enjoying my parents' company would have been understandable and certainly would have been more enjoyable. But in that instance it made a wonderful difference in my life to have done the right thing at the right time in the right way.

Let me close by citing again Alma's straightforward counsel to Corianton. With all the encouragement a father would want to give a son or daughter, he said that in the Resurrection the faithful are raised to a state of "endless happiness" wherein they "inherit the kingdom of God."[19] At that time, he said, we will be "raised to happiness according to [our] desires of happiness."[20] But he also sternly cautions: "Do not suppose . . . that [without repentance] ye shall be restored from sin to happiness. Behold, I say unto you, *wickedness never was happiness.*"[21] Sin is the antithesis of living "after the manner of happiness." Indeed those who believe otherwise, Alma says, "are without God in the world, and . . . have gone contrary to the nature of God; therefore, they are in a state contrary to the nature of happiness."[22]

A state contrary to the nature of happiness. That is the worst state I can imagine to live in. I invite you to rejoice in any state you have ever been in—Arizona, Rhode Island, Tennessee, Wisconsin—*any* state except the "state contrary to the nature of happiness." I ask you to reject transgression in order to live consistent with the nature of God, which is the nature of true happiness. I encourage you and applaud you in pursuing the path that leads to it. You can't find it any other way.

NOTES

From a talk given at a BYU–Idaho devotional, September 23, 2014.

1. *Teachings of the Prophet Joseph Smith,* sel. Joseph Fielding Smith (1976), 255.

2. Aristotle, *The Nicomachean Ethics.* With an English translation by H. Rackham (1982).

3. Henry David Thoreau, http://www.goodreads.com/quotes/146930-i -am-a-happy-camper-so-i-guess-i-m-doing.

4. Matthew 19:30; see also Matthew 10:39.

5. 2 Nephi 5:27.

6. James E. Faust, "Our Search for Happiness," *Ensign,* October 2000, 2.

7. John 14:5–6, 13–14.

8. David O. McKay, in Conference Report, October 1919, 180; emphasis added.

9. Quoted by Dr. Frank Crane, *Syracuse Herald* of Syracuse, New York, January 1, 1914.

10. Doctrine and Covenants 121:45–46.

11. Doctrine and Covenants 64:34.

12. Elizabeth Gilbert, *Eat, Pray, Love* (2006).

13. Gilbert, *Eat, Pray, Love.*

14. Mother Teresa, http://www.goodreads.com/quotes/33359-let-no-one -ever-come-to-you-without-leaving-better.

15. 3 Nephi 11:29.

16. Lynn G. Robbins, "Agency and Anger," *Ensign,* May 1998, 80.

17. 2 Nephi 5:17.

18. 2 Nephi 5:24.

19. Alma 41:4.

20. Alma 41:5.

21. Alma 41:10; emphasis added.

22. Alma 41:11.

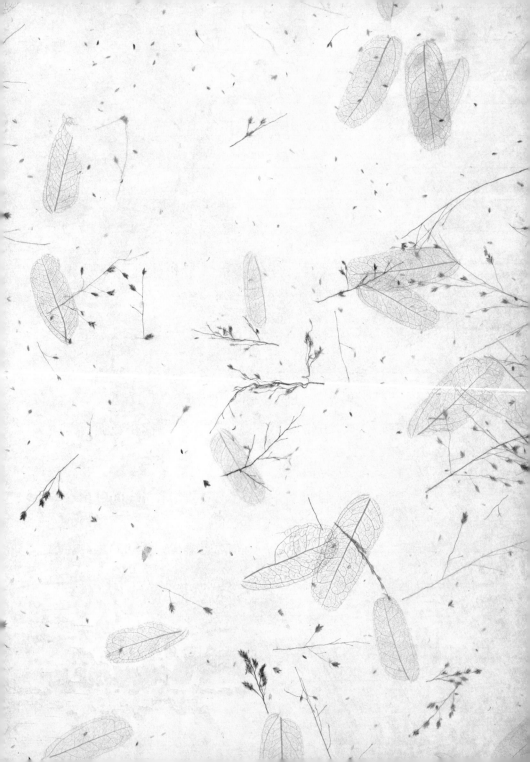

Love. HEALING.

HELP. Hope.

THE POWER OF CHRIST

to counter all troubles in all times—

including the end of times.

THAT IS THE SAFE HARBOR GOD WANTS FOR

US IN PERSONAL OR PUBLIC DAYS OF DESPAIR.

To my friends who
seek strength in the last days

— ⁓ —

CHAPTER 19

SAFETY FOR THE SOUL

Prophecies regarding the last days often refer to large-scale calamities such as earthquakes or famines or floods. These in turn may be linked to widespread economic or political upheavals of one kind or another.

But there is one kind of latter-day destruction that has always sounded to me more personal than public, more individual than collective—a warning, perhaps more applicable inside the Church than outside it. The Savior warned that in the last days even those of the covenant, the very elect, could be deceived by the enemy of truth.[1] If we think of this as a form of spiritual destruction, it may cast light on another latter-day prophecy. Think of the heart as the figurative center of our faith, the poetic location of our loyalties and our values; then consider Jesus's declaration that in the last days "men's hearts [shall fail] them."[2]

The encouraging thing, of course, is that our Father in Heaven knows all of these latter-day dangers, these troubles of the heart and soul, and has given counsel and protections regarding them.

In light of that, it has always been significant to me that the Book of Mormon, one of the Lord's powerful keystones[3] in this counteroffensive against latter-day ills, begins with a great parable of life, an extended allegory of hope versus fear, of light versus darkness, of salvation versus destruction.

In Lehi's dream an already difficult journey gets more difficult when a mist of darkness arises, obscuring any view of the safe but narrow path his family and others are to follow. It is imperative to note that this mist of darkness descends on *all* the travelers—the faithful and the determined ones (the elect, we might even say) as well as the weaker and ungrounded ones. The principal point of the story is that the successful travelers resist all distractions, including the lure of forbidden paths and jeering taunts from the vain and proud who have taken those paths. The record says that the protected "did press their way forward, continually [and, I might add, tenaciously] holding fast" to a rod of iron that runs unfailingly along the course of the true path.[4] However dark the night *or* the day, the rod marks the way of that solitary, redeeming trail.

"I beheld," Nephi says later, "that the rod of iron . . . was the word of God, [leading] . . . to the tree of life; . . . a representation of the love of God." Viewing this manifestation of God's love, Nephi goes on to say:

"I looked and beheld the Redeemer of the world, . . . [who] went forth ministering unto the people. . . .

" . . . And I beheld multitudes of people who were sick, and who were afflicted with all manner of diseases, and with devils and unclean spirits; . . . and they were healed by the power of the Lamb of God; and the devils and the unclean spirits were cast out."[5]

Love. Healing. Help. Hope. The power of Christ to counter all troubles in all times—including the end of times. That is the safe harbor God wants for us in personal or public days of despair. That is the message with which the Book of Mormon begins, and that is the message with which it ends, calling all to "come unto Christ, and be perfected in him."[6] That phrase—taken from Moroni's final lines of testimony, written thousand years after Lehi's vision—is a dying man's testimony of the only true way.

May I refer to a modern "last days" testimony? When Joseph Smith and his brother Hyrum started for Carthage to face what they knew would be an imminent martyrdom, Hyrum read these words to comfort the heart of his brother:

"Thou hast been faithful; wherefore . . . thou shalt be made strong, even unto the sitting down in the place which I have prepared in the mansions of my Father.

"And now I, Moroni, bid farewell . . . until we shall meet before the judgment-seat of Christ."[7]

A few short verses from the twelfth chapter of Ether in the Book of Mormon. Before closing the book, Hyrum turned down the corner of the page from which he had read, marking it as part of the everlasting testimony for which these two brothers were about to die. I have held in my hand that book, the very copy from which Hyrum read, the same corner of the page turned down, still visible. Later, when actually incarcerated in the jail, Joseph the Prophet turned to the guards who held him captive and bore a powerful testimony of the divine authenticity of the Book of Mormon.[8] Shortly thereafter pistol and ball would take the lives of these two testators.

As one of a thousand elements of my own testimony of the divinity of the Book of Mormon, I submit this as yet one more evidence of its truthfulness. In this their greatest—and last—hour of need, I ask you: would these men blaspheme before God by continuing to fix their lives, their honor, and their own search for eternal salvation on a book (and by implication a church and a ministry) they had fictitiously created out of whole cloth?

Never mind that their wives are about to be widows and their children fatherless. Never mind that their little band of followers will yet be "houseless, friendless and homeless" and that their children will leave footprints of blood across frozen rivers and an untamed prairie floor.[9] Never mind that legions will die and other legions live declaring in the four quarters of this earth that they know the Book of Mormon and the Church which espouses it to be true. Disregard all of that, and tell me whether in this hour of death these two men would enter the presence of their Eternal Judge quoting from and finding solace in a book which, if *not* the very word of God, would brand them as imposters and charlatans until the end of time? *They would not do that!* They were willing to die rather than deny the divine origin and the eternal truthfulness of the Book of Mormon.

For more than 180 years this book has been examined and attacked, denied and deconstructed, targeted and torn apart like perhaps no other book in modern religious history—perhaps like no other book in *any* religious history. And still it stands. Failed theories about its origins have been born and parroted and have died—from Ethan Smith to Solomon Spaulding to deranged paranoid to cunning genius. None of these frankly pathetic answers for this book has ever withstood examination because *there is no other answer* than the one Joseph gave as its young unlearned translator. In this I stand with my own great-grandfather, who said simply enough, "No wicked man could write such a book as this; and no good man would write it, unless it were true and he were commanded of God to do so."[10]

I testify that one cannot come to full faith in this latter-day work—and thereby find the fullest measure of peace and comfort in these, our times—until he or she embraces the divinity of the Book of Mormon and the Lord Jesus Christ, of whom it testifies. If *anyone* is foolish enough or misled enough to reject 531 pages of a heretofore unknown text teeming with literary and Semitic complexity without honestly attempting to account for the origin of those pages—especially without accounting for their powerful witness of Jesus Christ and the profound spiritual impact that witness has had on what is now tens of millions of readers—if that is the case, then such a person, elect or otherwise, has been deceived; and if he or she leaves this Church, it must be done by crawling over or under or around the Book of Mormon to make that exit. In that sense the book is what Christ Himself was said to be: "a stone of stumbling, . . . a rock of offence,"[11] a barrier in the path of one who wishes not to believe in this work. Witnesses, even witnesses who were for a time hostile to Joseph, testified to their death that they had seen an angel and had handled the plates. "They have been shown unto us by the power of God, and not of man," they declared. "Wherefore we know of a surety that the work is true."[12]

Now, I did not sail with the brother of Jared in crossing an ocean, settling in a new world. I did not hear King Benjamin speak his angelically delivered sermon. I did not proselyte with Alma and Amulek nor witness the fiery death of innocent believers. I was not among the Nephite crowd who touched the wounds of the resurrected Lord, nor did I weep with Mormon and Moroni over the destruction of an entire civilization. But my testimony of this record and the peace it brings to the human heart is as binding and unequivocal as was theirs. Like them, "[I] give [my name] unto the world, to witness unto the world that which [I] *have seen*." And like them, "[I] lie not, God bearing witness of it."[13]

I ask that my testimony of the Book of Mormon and all that it implies, given under my own oath and office, be recorded by men on earth and angels in heaven. I hope I have a few years left in my "last days," but whether I do or do not, I want it absolutely clear when I stand before the judgment bar of God that I declared to the world, in the most straightforward language I could summon, that the Book of Mormon is true, that it came forth the way Joseph said it came forth and was given to bring happiness and hope to the faithful in the travail of the latter days.

My witness echoes that of Nephi, who wrote part of the book in *his* "last days":

"Hearken unto these words and believe in Christ; and if ye believe not in these words believe in Christ. *And if ye shall believe in Christ ye will believe in these words, for they are the words of Christ*, . . . and they teach all men that they should do good.

"And if they are not the words of Christ, judge ye—for Christ will show unto you, with power and great glory, that they are his words, *at the last day*."[14]

God always provides safety for the soul, and with the Book of Mormon, He has again done that in our time. Remember this declaration by Jesus Himself: "Whoso treasureth up my word, shall not be deceived"[15]—and in the last days neither your heart nor your faith will fail you.

NOTES

From a talk given at general conference, October 2009.

1. See Matthew 24:24; see also Joseph Smith—Matthew 1:22.
2. Luke 21:26.
3. See Joseph Smith, *History of the Church of Jesus Christ of Latter-day Saints,* 7 vols. (1932–1951), 4:461.
4. 1 Nephi 8:30.
5. 1 Nephi 11:25, 27–28, 31.
6. Moroni 10:32.
7. Ether 12:37–38; see also Doctrine and Covenants 135:5.
8. See Smith, *History of the Church,* 6:600.
9. Smith, *History of the Church,* 4:539.
10. George Cannon, quoted in "The Twelve Apostles," in Andrew Jenson, ed., *The Historical Record,* 6:175.
11. 1 Peter 2:8.
12. "The Testimony of Three Witnesses," Book of Mormon.
13. "The Testimony of Eight Witnesses," Book of Mormon; emphasis added.
14. 2 Nephi 33:10–11; emphasis added.
15. Joseph Smith—Matthew 1:37.

WE MUST
TRUST GOD,

including trusting what He does with us, knowing

He is making something that will be not only to

His glory but finally to ours as well.

To our friends
in the covenant

———⌒———

CHAPTER 20

CONSIDERING COVENANTS: WOMEN, MEN, PERSPECTIVE, PROMISES

JEFFREY R. HOLLAND AND PATRICIA T. HOLLAND

JRH We are very aware of the differing circumstances in which the women of the Church find themselves. Among our sisters there are those who have not married, who are divorced, who are widowed, who are raising children alone, who are childless, and so on.

PTH Whatever your circumstance, we ask for the peace of the gospel to be in your hearts and in your lives. The Prophet Joseph Smith once wrote, "[The Holy Ghost] is . . . powerful in expanding the mind, enlightening the understanding, and storing the intellect with present knowledge. . . . As it falls upon the . . . seed of Abraham, it is calm and serene."[1] May we be "calm and serene" as we all try to expand our minds and enlighten our understanding.

JRH Among the most important testimonies I could bear is that of God's love for you. I wish to stress at some length that God is good, as any father worthy of the name will always be to his children. That fact has important implications for our making and keeping covenants. I worry that many sometimes feel too detached from God, seem too convinced that there is too great a distance between Kolob and Kanab. You fear that God in His heaven, with all of His urgent national and international, galactic and intergalactic business, is certain to be occupied with things other than your hopes and happiness. Well, I do not know exactly how He does it but my testimony is that He does know us and does love us and that He hears our personal prayers. My testimony is that *nothing* in this universe is more important to Him than your hopes and happiness. Nephi wrote, "The Lord God . . . doeth not anything save it be for the benefit of the world. . . . He inviteth them all to come unto him and partake of his goodness."[2] When we pass through the veil, it will be thrilling to learn how God watches over us and cares for us, how He knows our every thought. For now it is enough to know simply that He does it. The Prophet Joseph taught that we could not fully exercise faith in

God until we understood His nature.[3] It really shouldn't need to be stressed that God is good, but sometimes in our extremity we seem to forget that. Through the cunning influence of the adversary, we have lost something of that most encouraging doctrine down through the ages.

PTH That aspect of God's character may be the single most important point to make when we are considering covenants. God wants us to be happy! He is eternally committed to our well-being and wants us to be committed to it as well. The safety and surety of making covenants with God is anchored in the fact that He has prepared them for our exquisite joy. He won't hurt us, He won't trick us, He won't disparage or demean us. No one will be left alone or adrift or unanchored. Goodness in God means exactly what it means in us (only in His case even more so)—living up to the highest ideal, living up to the best that He is.

JRH In an instructive moment from the Book of Mormon, you will recall that Ammon had been teaching King Lamoni the gospel, specifically the eternal plan of salvation or, as Alma would later call it, "the great plan of happiness."[4] As this plan was presented to his mind and to his heart, the beauty, safety, and protection of God's love and Christ's selfless sacrifice overwhelmed him. In that moment, Lamoni cried out, "O Lord, have mercy [upon me]; according to thy abundant mercy,"[5] and he fell to the earth as if he were dead.

PTH After two days his servants were preparing to bury the king, certain not only that he was dead but that his body was beginning to decay. His wife, the queen, believing this missionary could do it, asked Ammon to work a miracle, specifically to raise her husband from this deathlike state he was in. I have always been touched that it was a wife, a woman, who stepped forward at a crucial moment and exerted such faith in behalf of her husband. In doing so, she brought a major turning point in Book of Mormon history. Ammon would later say of her, "Woman, there has not been such great faith among all the people of the Nephites."[6]

JRH The record says: "Now, this was what Ammon desired, for he knew that king Lamoni was under the power of God; he knew that the dark veil of unbelief was being cast away from his mind, and the light which did light up his mind, which was the light of the glory of God, *which was a marvelous light of his goodness*—yea, this light had infused such joy into his soul, the cloud of darkness having been dispelled, and that the light of everlasting life was lit up in his soul, yea, he knew that this had overcome his natural frame, and he was carried away in God."[7]

PTH The light that comes into our lives in times of great personal need, the light that dispels the clouds of darkness and rends the veil of unbelief, the light that lit up Lamoni's mind to the point of spiritual transcendence and physical collapse is *the marvelous light of God's goodness*. It is the realization of such divine compassion, mercy, and long-suffering that lifts those oppressive clouds from our lives. It is His goodness—goodness that gives us a plan of safety and happiness, goodness that gives us a Redeeming Brother even at unspeakable Parental cost, goodness that gives us help in times of daily struggle and nightly sorrow. The glory of such compassion lights up the soul and wrenches away fear, anger, and disbelief so majestically that we have to be, in effect, carried from the scene.

JRH   That is why we can make covenants with such confidence, knowing with certainty God's power over darkness and danger and troubles of every kind. We should give gratitude from the depths of our soul for "a plan of happiness" that provides for escape from every personal mistake we have ever made and every dumb thing we have ever done. We should express eternal thanks for the pure, single-minded, divine goodness that can cover every concern, heal every wound, make up for every defect, and eventually dry every tear. That's the God and Christ and plan King Lamoni saw, and that is what stunned him so. It will stun us, too—by its strength and by its splendor—when our need is great enough, our faith strong enough, and our view clear enough to see it. In our hour of extremity we will, if we keep our covenants, see the clouds of darkness lift, the dark veil of unbelief cast away by the hand of a Father who is eternally committed to our happiness.

PTH There are in life a thousand and one challenges that can try our faith, or at least try our faithfulness. Some days it can be hard to keep going, particularly if we are already weary from long effort and most particularly if we feel we are struggling on alone. My testimony to you is that God has not forsaken you and will never forsake you. That is one of the reasons our theme of covenants and the keeping of them is so crucial, so central to the mortal experience. Covenants are vital not only because they commit us to being unshakable in our devotion to God, which they do, but perhaps even more encouragingly, they remind us God will always be unshakable in His devotion toward us. And though we may falter and make some mistakes, He never falters. He never makes a mistake. He is ever faithful to us. That is the beauty and majesty inherent in the covenants we make with God.

JRH Covenants are binding, supernal, consummate contracts between God and His children. They are the solemn promises of Deity—a God who always keeps His word—that heaven will pour out unmeasured blessings upon all who are faithful and honor the conditions of their pledge. An individual can swear an oath, but only when God reciprocates in kind is there a covenant established.

We know that oaths are never to be spoken lightly, and covenantal language is of a higher order yet. By definition, covenants invoke the most sacred language we can utter in this world. It is a language that establishes a bond and a relationship unique in the human experience. It is the means by which a fallen family make their way back to eternal splendor. It is the means by which each one of us can be, in the Lord's own words, "a peculiar treasure unto me above all people."[8] That is why keeping our covenants will, as the scripture says, add "glory . . . upon their heads for ever and ever."[9]

On those days when we think life is harder to bear than we can endure, and when we may think God has somehow forgotten us, that is the time most of all when we should remember our covenants. When God wants to remind us of the surety and permanence of our blessings, He speaks of sealing them or binding them or (as Joseph Smith once said we might speak of it) as welding them.[10] These are muscular verbs. It is intended to be a strong message. He uses the most powerful terms in our language when asking us to keep our promises and to believe He will keep His.

PTH This may all seem like belaboring the obvious because probably no one reading this has ever believed that God was anything but good. But then why do we so often feel, or at least say we feel, that God has forsaken us or has forgotten us or is unmindful of our concerns? Do we ever, even fleetingly, resent God or get angry with Him or determine not to hear His voice? "Not my will, but thine, be done"[11] is only possible for us to say—and mean—if we understand that God is totally committed to our happiness.

That is why Christ was very careful to say that He was a "good" shepherd, not a bad or mediocre one.[12] Bad shepherds lose their sheep and forget to feed them and leave them vulnerable to wolves and weather. But not Christ, and not His Father. If we will just agree to be part of the flock—by covenant—then we have Their promise that we will never be forsaken or forgotten, never be left on our own. In the end the promise is that Christ gave everything, including His life, for His sheep. That is the earthly counterpart to the same heavenly loyalty God the Father has always given to us.

JRH   This is particularly important to remember when we are not so much dissatisfied with God as we are dissatisfied with ourselves—and then blame Him for it. So often we do not like the way we are or the way we look or the way we feel. We think we are weak and worthless and have made too many mistakes. Sometimes we don't remain faithful because we think we are beyond the grasp of divine help. We long to be like someone else who is less feeble, someone who has, we think, greater gifts of appearance or education or talent or opportunity. We grow discontented with ourselves, and then faith in everything else starts to falter. But we would certainly be happier if we understood that we are God's handiwork, divine art produced at His potter's wheel, and we must believe He is making that which is best and most beautiful for us. We must trust God, including trusting what He does with us, knowing He is making something that will be not only to His glory but finally to ours as well. We can expect perfectly satisfactory explanations later about disappointments we may have experienced along the way.

My point is that it can be spiritually fatal to think wrongly about God. Such dim views of the light of God's goodness can immediately affect how we see not only ourselves but also His Church, His Church governance, His Church leaders, and our neighbors in and out of the Church. It can certainly affect how we see spouses, children, marriage, and other family matters. Wrong thinking about God can lead to a terrible breach, a severe separation, an ever wider gulf of doubt and unbelief. It can sap our strength as dramatically as does sin. This is why the first great commandments in both the Old and New Testaments ask us to focus on the true nature of God, specifically His love and compassion. Surely our erroneous, ungenerous views of God's love are every bit as wrong and idolatrous as creating a gold calf or some other world-class graven image.

PTH It seems to me obvious (though still not so easy to do) that submitting to God's will would be infinitely less difficult if we could accept the fact that He is longing to bless us, that His only desire is for our happiness. This realization can be a blinding, stupefying experience, as King

Lamoni reminds us, but then we would not only submit gladly, we would enthusiastically embrace His will. We would greet His counsel and commandments with delight. Our hearts would spring out to meet them.

JRH In what I consider one of the more remarkable testimonies shared by one of our BYU faculty members, Professor Bruce Young speaks of the "miracle" it was for him to find a wife and to now be so thoroughly happy in marriage. Shakespeare scholar that he is, Bruce notes the problem in *The Winter's Tale* of one who sees his marriage breaking apart because he does not believe that anything, including his good and gracious wife, can really be this marvelous. Surely there must be something wrong somewhere. Surely we weren't really meant to be happy. Surely God is a trickster and must be waiting to jerk the rug from beneath us very soon now. With such suspicion and self-interest destined to destroy virtually any life or marriage, the character is told that the marriage can be redeemed, but only upon one unyielding, fundamental obligation. "It is required [that you] awake your faith," he is told.

PTH Brother Young then observed that it was just such lack of faith—so much fear, and suspicion, and doubt—that had kept him from getting married. He had friends whose marriages hadn't worked out, so what guarantee was there for him? Would he marry the wrong person? Would she eventually, or worse yet immediately, stop loving him? The fears of two decades came to terrify him as the possibility of marriage seemed more and more imminent. Then this key to his happiness, which continues to this day: "I let go," he said, "of my great burden of preconceptions, judgments, anticipations, and concerns, and became—in at least one respect—as a little child." The first step, he said, was to believe in the possibility of good things—surely one of the greatest of all children's virtues. Children believe everything is possible and they believe everything will be good.

One of our challenges in making and keeping covenants is overcoming this kind of resistance we have to our own happiness. Yielding on such matters is often a painful, long-term process requiring us to take responsibility for the confusion, fears, and resentment we feel, realizing they are largely of our own making. But we must give them up—a hard thing for all of us who want to cling to everything we have ever created.

JRH Such worries, fears, anxieties, such self-torment and self-pity, set up overwhelming, potentially unyielding barriers to our happiness. They distance us from God and they distance us from each other—from spouses, children, friends, almost everyone, and they keep us from seeing God's plan as it really is and ought to be.

Brother Young found himself resisting love, avoiding commitment, fearing disappointment and betrayal of a dozen kinds, all of which became for him a sort of miserable protection against the possibility of real happiness.

"Having experienced such self-created conflict," he concludes, "I am struck by how closely critics of the Church resemble people upset with their marriage partners. There is, for both the critics and the dissatisfied spouses, the same combination of inexorable logic and essential blindness. Everything they see seems obvious to them. . . . But anesthetized to their own faults, [while] hypersensitive to the imperfections of others, they do not see the real and potential splendor in [those] with whom they are yoked. The dark things they see are too often the products of their own hearts. And the evidence of a spouse's willingness to love and give, like the abundant evidence of God's love and active presence in His Church, is easily ignored or forgotten."[13]

PTH If we are willing to receive and remember it, there is always an abundance of evidence to sustain our faith, not only in a loyal husband or wife, but in the Church and its leaders and in the reality and love and goodness of God. Love, marriage, and friendships of a hundred kinds are like membership in the Church. They require at the outset—and all the way through—an act of faith in that which will bless and save us in the end. That is why covenants are so dearly and deeply important. We claim through them the promise that the darkness of night will disappear, that questions will be answered, and in the final day, all will be well with us.

JRH With that trust in God and the love we really must feel for each other as we make our way toward the celestial city, I wish to make something of an appeal to the women of the kingdom.

I thank you for the service you render to your families, to the Church, and to the neighborhoods and communities in which you live. You do this day in and day out, with large families or small families or no families at all. Yours is a divine touch, and your history has been the history of compassion, of conviction, of strength and stability.

PTH President Howard W. Hunter reminded us that the Savior particularly appreciated the company and comfort of women. And perhaps it is true that the women and children sensed more keenly who and what He truly was, more so perhaps than some of the harder men of the day. Women remained to the very last, lingering in view of the cross—"many women,"[14] the gospels record—ministering unto Him as best they could, and it was the women who followed faithfully to mark where the Savior's body was laid. Of course it was to Mary that Christ first appeared as the resurrected Lord, and it was she to whom He entrusted the delivery of the glorious message to His disciples that He had risen. Quoting President Hunter:

"As our Lord and Savior needed the women of his time for a comforting hand, a listening ear, a believing heart, a kind look, an encouraging word, loyalty—even in his hour of humiliation, agony, and death—so we, his servants all across the Church, need you, the women of the Church, to stand with us and for us in stemming the tide of evil that threatens to engulf us. Together we must stand faithful and firm in the faith against superior numbers of other-minded people. It seems to me that there is a great need to rally the women of the Church to stand with and for the Brethren in stemming the tide of evil that surrounds us and in moving forward the work of our Savior. . . . Obedient to him we are a majority. But only together can we accomplish the work he has given us to do and be prepared for the day when we shall see him."[15]

JRH It is as Martin Luther once said, "The kingdom of God is like a besieged city surrounded on all sides by death. Each man [and woman] has [a] place on the wall to defend and no one can stand where another stands, but nothing prevents us from calling encouragement to one another."[16]

I think the Brethren have seen some spiritual death near the gates of the city in past days and perhaps they fear they will see more in the years ahead. This is an invitation to each of us to take our place on the wall and to call out encouragement to one another. I have my station and Sister Holland has hers, and each of you has your own. None of us will stand in the place of any other, but like Gideon's valiant band,[17] we can each stand in our own place. We can stand together in a fight against the prince of darkness and the dangers of spiritual decay. Our covenants are our protection. Our strength will be in the Lord. Every woman, man, and accountable child will be enlisted before "the conflict is o'er."[18] We must stand true and call out encouragement to one another.

In Civil War days a performer named Blondin astonished the nation by crossing the Niagara River on a tightrope. President Abraham Lincoln, facing a delegation of critics, said:

"Gentlemen, suppose all the property you possessed were in gold, and you had placed it in the hands of a Blondin to carry across the Niagara River on a rope. With slow, cautious steps he walks to the rope, bearing your all. Would you shake the cable and keep shouting at him, 'Blondin, stand up a little straighter; Blondin, stoop a little more; go a little faster; lean more to the south; lean a little more to the north?' Would that be your behaviour in such an emergency?

"No, you would hold your breath, every one of you, as well as your tongues. You would keep your hands off until he was safe on the other side.

"This government, gentlemen, is carrying an immense weight. Untold treasures are in its hands. The persons managing the ship of state in this storm are doing the best they can. Don't worry them with needless warnings and complaints. . . . Be patient, and we will get you safe[ly] across."[19]

PTH In that same spirit, the leaders of our Church carry an immense weight, and with our support they will get us safely through. I believe the Brethren are looking to the women of the Church, the strong, valiant, ever-faithful women of the Church, to be defenders of priesthood power. In times of difficulty and stress ahead, it will be the women of the Church—as well as the men—who will speak persuasively of God's plan, of His eternal government, and of His priesthood assignments. *In the years ahead, some of the great defenders of priesthood roles for men will be women speaking to other women.* A woman can speak to another woman in language they would not normally use and with a fervor men would not dare invoke. God has a view of women, who they are, what they do incomparably, and what eternally they will be. Women must seize that vision and embrace it, or they—and the human family with them—will perish.

JRH There has been much confusion—or at least much discussion—of late about gender and rights and priesthood. In the *Young Woman's Journal* of 1914, Elder James E. Talmage wrote a remarkable piece, particularly so given the date of its publication. It could have been written today. Noting the sacred and eternal role of both women and men, Elder Talmage said a century ago, "The status of woman in the world is a subject of present-day discussion and an element of current social unrest; it is, however, by no means a new topic. . . . [Woman] has suffered the greatest humiliation during periods of spiritual darkness, when the Gospel of Christ was forgotten. [But in the light of the gospel] woman occupies a position all her own in the eternal economy of the Creator; and in that position she is as truly superior to man as is he to her in his appointed place. Woman shall yet come to her own, exercising her rights and her privileges as a sanctified investiture which none shall dare profane."

PTH Of this equal honor but eternal distinction between men and women, Elder Talmage goes on to say: "In every organization, however simple or complex, there must needs be a centralization of authority, in short, a head. [God has placed man at the head of the household, alongside his wife as full and faithful partner], and God holds him accountable for his administration. That many men fail in their station, that some are weak and unfit, that in particular instances the wife may be the more capable and in divers ways the better of the pair, should not be considered as evidence . . . of unrighteousness in the established [order]. Woman should be regarded, not in the sense of privilege but of right, as the associate of man in the . . . home, and they two should form the governing head of the family institution, which to each separately pertain duties and function which the other is less qualified to discharge. Weakness or inefficiency on the part of either in specified instances must not be taken to impugn the wisdom by which the organization of the home and of society has been planned [by God]."

JRH Continuing, Elder Talmage says, "In the restored Church of Jesus Christ, the Holy Priesthood is conferred, as an individual bestowal, upon men only, and this in accordance with Divine requirement. It is not given to woman to exercise the authority of the priesthood independently; nevertheless, in the sacred endowments associated with the ordinances [of] the House of the Lord, [it is clear how dramatically] woman shares with man the blessings of the priesthood. When the frailties and imperfection of mortality are left behind, in the glorified state of the blessed hereafter, husband and wife will administer in their respective stations, seeing and understanding alike, and cooperating to the full in the government of their family kingdom. Then shall woman be recompensed in rich measure for all the injustice that womanhood has endured in mortality. Then shall woman reign by Divine right, a queen in the resplendent realm of her glorified state, even as exalted man shall stand, priest and king unto the Most High God. Mortal eye cannot see nor mind comprehend the beauty, glory, and majesty of a righteous woman made perfect in the celestial kingdom of God."[20]

PTH That is a powerful and impressive discourse of nearly a century ago. It reaffirms my faith that the Brethren know very well the issues of the day—in ours and every other era of the Church. I wish I could adequately share with you my conviction about the government of God we all enjoy at the hand of God. We have been blessed by it in our home, and we have been blessed by it in this Church. I pay tribute to the prophets, seers, and revelators who say to us that women are invited to exercise their rights and privileges "as a sanctified investiture which none shall dare profane." I believe deeply that "mortal eye cannot see nor mind comprehend the beauty, glory, and majesty of a righteous woman made perfect in the celestial kingdom of God."

JRH As the Prophet Joseph Smith continually taught, in this Church we *do* believe in a government and kingdom that ultimately is not of this world. Ours will not be a democracy or an oligarchy. Technically it will not even be a theocracy. It will be, in the millennial day, a monarchy, with Christ reigning as King of kings and Lord of lords. Of that government Joseph's principal student, Brigham Young—who so strenuously taught us to prepare for the government of God and tried to his dying day to implement it—said: "This is the government of God. A perfect system of government—a kingdom of Gods and angels and all beings who will submit themselves to that government. There is no other true government in heaven or upon the earth."[21]

PTH As perfect as the government of God is, none of us as mortal participants in it are perfect. Women can certainly be damaging to men, but at the same time it should never be said of any Latter-day Saint man that he contributed to the "injustice that womanhood has endured in mortality," to use Elder Talmage's searing phrase. Perhaps too many have yet to grasp the profound seriousness of that Liberty Jail revelation which emphasized that "No power or influence can or ought to be maintained by virtue of the priesthood, only by persuasion, by long-suffering, by gentleness and meekness, and by love unfeigned."[22]

This will embarrass him, but I am expressing it anyway. My husband has truly tried to live his life "by love unfeigned" and to treat his wife and children with dignity, respect, and deference. There has been no greater joy in my life than living with a man who tries to love and respect me in the spirit of section 121. That has been so rewarding and fulfilling to me that when it then gets down to priesthood matters, I have been very happy to give him that same deference and respect.

JRH I am flattered by Sister Holland's expression, but in all honesty I must say that my priesthood bearing has not yet matched the power of her personal purity. I can honestly say I have never known anyone with higher motives or deeper belief. She has trusted in God all her life and has willingly trusted in me.

In the spirit of that debt I owe to Pat, the Prophet Joseph said, "It is the duty of a husband to love, cherish, and nourish his wife, and cleave unto her and none else. He ought to honor her as himself, and he ought to regard her feeling with tenderness. . . . [He] is not to rule over his wife as a tyrant, neither as one who is fearful or jealous that his wife will get out of her place and prevent him from exercising his authority. It is his duty to be a man of God—for a man of God is a man of wisdom—ready at all times to obtain from the scriptures, the revelations, and from on high, such instruction as are necessary for the edification and salvation of his household."[23]

PTH Unfortunately, not all men measure up to their assignment, but we stand with the prophets in saying the principles are true and the ultimate, ideal government of God is perfect. So we need to stay with our beliefs until— even if it is, as Elder Talmage says, "in the blessed hereafter"—we fully realize and see clearly the exalted, ideal and perfect glory of women and men crowned with equal majesty in their heavenly reward.

JRH It will be no surprise to anyone that much of the concern I hear from women on these contemporary issues comes because of the failure of some men. But please, to remedy this we don't throw the baby out with the bathwater, we don't retreat from or alter what has been declared as the perfect government of God. One day, and we pray sooner rather than later, we will enjoy the perfect peace that surpasses understanding—in gender issues as well as every other matter that human inadequacy may cause.

PTH As BYU Professor Alma Don Sorensen has written, "It must be admitted, as some of our critics claim, that sex discrimination exists among LDS people more or less as it does in the societies surrounding them. But the explanation for this discrimination does not lie at all in the belief system of the restored gospel but in the fact that we live too much in the world and fail to realize the equality between men and women that living in the kingdom requires. The fact is that the doctrines and principles of the kingdom are the proper remedy for the unequal treatment of the sexes . . . not its cause."[24]

If we can help one another with our limitations in a marriage or in a family or in the Church, and not retreat from nor do damage to the very truths, principles, and covenants that will one day thrill us and fulfill us and empower us beyond measure, then we will—both women and men—find that we have successfully traveled the path of progression from womanhood and manhood to Godhood. Then we can sit enthroned "crowned with glory and majesty" like (and these are Elder Talmage's words) the "eternal Father and the eternal Mother."

JRH These are not tranquil times, nor are they for the fainthearted. But then we have just learned from Elder Talmage that 1914 was not so smooth a period either, and neither were those days along the Sweetwater and the Platte and the frozen passes of Wyoming. But President Spencer W. Kimball spoke for all the difficult seasons of the Saints when he said, "To be a righteous woman is a glorious thing in any age. To be a righteous woman during the winding up scenes on this earth, before the second coming of our Savior, is an especially noble calling. The righteous woman's strength and influence today can be tenfold what it might be in more tranquil times. She has been placed here to help to enrich, to protect, and to guard the home—which is society's basic and most noble institution. Other institutions in society may falter and even fail, but the righteous woman can help to save the home, which may be the last and only sanctuary some mortals know in the midst of storm and strife. . . . We have grown strong as a people because our mothers and our women have [made us so]. That ennobling quality must not be lost, even though some of the people of the world may try to persuade otherwise."[25]

PTH   May I claim a moment of personal privilege on President Kimball's thought about saving home and children. I have always wanted to speak somewhere to someone about being a mother. I have been pressed into service in a variety of ways in this work, just as you have. And I have been blessed all along the way, just as you have.

But I would like to say here that all I have ever really wanted to be is a mother. I was thrust into the public eye during our years at BYU, and I fulfilled those public assignments. It was my duty, and they were wonderful years. Even now, as the wife of a General Authority, my life is more public than I prefer. But my husband's calling is an unequaled and profound privilege for our family. We have never been more blessed in our lives. But all I have ever wanted to be is a mother, to have, as the Psalmist said, a "quiver full" of children.[26] Such was not to be our lot in life. We were blessed with three perfect children, and then I suppose Heavenly Father felt He could not improve on those three, so the others we had hoped for never came.

But as long as we are speaking of ideals and blessings to come in the great beyond, my happiest thoughts and my highest hopes are to someday, somewhere, on some small green and grassy piece of God's celestial realm, sit with my children and grandchildren, crowded around me for as far as the eye can see, and tell them of the love I feel and speak of eternal things. I long for that sense of family and home, and it is the most motivating force in my life. I wanted it in our early married life, I want it now, and I want it in the world to come.

Our eleventh article of faith allows all to choose their religion and to worship as they wish. In that same spirit, if I may pursue the path I most long for and the one I hope to savor through eternity, I choose home and mothering and womanhood, now and forever.

JRH My responsibilities as a father are all that Sister Holland has suggested for mothers. It seems to me that if fathers would focus on their marriage, home, and family with anywhere near the intensity they focus on their careers, then we would not have nearly so many women trying so frantically to get away from that marriage, home, and family. As someone said recently, too many mothers in America are dead tired because too many fathers in America are deadbeats. I am not here to berate fathers, but I do believe God will hold us accountable for our performance as fathers, sons, and brothers, and not for how we did as doctors, lawyers, and corporate chiefs.

I pray I can do better in my role as husband and father, the task in life I reverence and cherish the most. I pray I can merit the love my wife and children have always given me. They mean more to me than life itself. I desperately want my children to see at least something in their earthly father that would encourage their belief in a dependable, compassionate, and loving God. Certainly my children's view of their earthly mother has already prepared them to behold the splendor and strength of their heavenly mother one day.

PTH I testify that as women of covenant, we can be a powerful force for righteousness in this world. I believe it is our nature to kindle spirituality and spiritual strength within every sphere of our influence. We are bearers of light, even as John saw the woman in his marvelous revelation,[27] and I know we can be the instrument for conveying that light from one realm to another and another and another. That is at the heart of our "sanctified investiture" which none shall dare profane. I pray we will reach out enthusiastically for our assignment and rejoice in our

God-given appointment. As we do so, we will enjoy divine rights and powers and privileges surpassing any other earthly satisfaction. That I know and of that I testify, in the beloved name of the Lord Jesus Christ.

JRH May God bless all of you in this the true and living Church of the true and living God. I bless you that you may feel the arms of His love and protection around you, and that His angels will be on your right hand and on your left to bear you up in time of need. I bless you that all of your deepest, heartfelt longings will be met, that all wounds will be healed, and that sweet peace will be yours now and forever. May you be majestically proud of your womanhood and may men always be respectful of it. I bless you and promise you that your covenants will be a source of strength and satisfaction and safety to you. Through keeping them we can all rejoice in the triumph of the Savior of the world—including His saving of our personal world and all we hold dear within it—in whose sacred name I testify, even Jesus Christ, amen.

NOTES

From a talk given April 28, 1994, at Brigham Young University Women's Conference.

1. *Teachings of the Prophet Joseph Smith,* sel. Joseph Fielding Smith (1976), 149–50.
2. 2 Nephi 26:23, 24, 33.
3. This is, for example, the basic premise for *Lectures on Faith* (1985).
4. Alma 42:8.

5. Alma 18:41.

6. Alma 19:10.

7. Alma 19:6, emphasis added.

8. Exodus 19:5.

9. Abraham 3:26.

10. See Doctrine and Covenants 128:18.

11. Luke 22:42.

12. John 10:14.

13. See Bruce Young's essay, "The Miracle of Faith, The Miracle of Love: Some Personal Reflections," in Philip L. Barlow, ed., *A Thoughtful Faith: Essays on Belief by Mormon Scholars* (1986), 259–76.

14. Matthew 27:55.

15. Howard W. Hunter, "To the Women of the Church," *Ensign,* November 1992, 96.

16. Martin Luther, as quoted in Lewis Spitz, *The Renaissance and Reformation Movements* (1971), 335.

17. See Judges 7:21.

18. "We Are All Enlisted," *Hymns of The Church of Jesus Christ of Latter-day Saints* (1985), no. 250.

19. John Wesley Hill, *Abraham Lincoln: Man of God* (1926), 402, as quoted in Boyd K. Packer, *The Holy Temple* (1980), 168.

20. James E. Talmage, "The Eternity of Sex," *Young Woman's Journal,* October 1914, 600–603.

21. Brigham Young, in *Journal of Discourses,* 26 vols. (1854–1886), 7:142–43.

22. Doctrine and Covenants 121:41.

23. Joseph Smith, in *Elder's Journal,* August 1838, 61–62.

24. Alma Don Sorensen, "No Respecter of Persons: Equality in the Kingdom," in *As Women of Faith* (1989), 52.

25. Spencer W. Kimball, "Privileges and Responsibilities of Sisters," *Ensign,* November 1978, 103–4.

26. Psalm 127:5.

27. See Revelation 12:1.

ONE OF THE GREAT CONSOLATIONS

OF OUR MORTALITY IS THAT BECAUSE

WALKED SUCH A LONG, LONELY PATH

utterly alone,

we do not have to do so.

*To my friends
who feel alone*

CHAPTER 21

NONE WERE WITH HIM

This message is directed in a special way to those who are alone or feel alone or, worse yet, feel abandoned. These might include those longing to be married, those who have lost a spouse, and those who have lost—or have never been blessed with—children. Our empathy embraces wives forsaken by their husbands, husbands whose wives have walked away, and children bereft of one or the other of their parents—or both. This group can find within its broad circumference a soldier far from home, a missionary in those first weeks of homesickness, or a father out of work, afraid the fear in his eyes will be visible to his family. In short it can include all of us at various times in our lives.

To all such, I speak of the loneliest journey ever made and the unending blessings it brought to all in the human family. I speak of the Savior's solitary task of shouldering alone the burden of our salvation. Rightly He would say: "I have trodden the winepress alone; and of the people there was none with me. . . . I looked, and there was none to help; and I wondered that there was none to uphold [me]."[1]

We know from scripture that Jesus's messianic arrival in Jerusalem on the Sunday preceding Passover was a great public moment. But eagerness to continue walking with Him would quickly begin to wane.

Soon enough He was arraigned before the Israelite leaders of the day—first Annas, the former high priest, then Caiaphas, the current high priest. In their rush to judgment these men and their councils declared their verdict quickly and angrily. "What further need have we of witnesses?" they cried. "He is [worthy] of death."[2]

With that He was brought before the gentile rulers in the land. Herod Antipas, the tetrarch of Galilee, interrogated Him once, and Pontius Pilate, the Roman governor in Judea, did so twice, the second time declaring to the crowd, "I, having examined him before you, have found no fault in this man."[3] Then, in an act as unconscionable as it was illogical, Pilate "scourged Jesus, [and] delivered him to be crucified."[4] Pilate's freshly washed hands could not have been more stained or more unclean.

Such ecclesiastical and political rejection became more

NONE WERE WITH HIM | 251

personal when the citizenry in the street turned against Jesus as well. It is one of the ironies of history that sitting with Jesus in prison was a *real* blasphemer, a murderer and revolutionary known as Barabbas, a name or title in Aramaic meaning "son of the father."[5] Free to release one prisoner in the spirit of the Passover tradition, Pilate asked the people, "Whether of the twain will ye that I release unto you?" They said, "Barabbas."[6] So one godless "son of the father" was set free while a truly divine Son of His Heavenly Father moved on to crucifixion.

This was also a telling time among those who knew Jesus more personally. The most difficult to understand in this group is Judas Iscariot. We know the divine plan required Jesus to be crucified, but it is wrenching to think that one of His special witnesses who sat at His feet, heard Him pray, watched Him heal, and felt His touch could betray Him and all that He was for thirty pieces of silver. Never in the history of this world has so little money purchased so much infamy. We are not the ones to judge Judas's fate, but Jesus said of His betrayer, "Good [were it] for that man if he had not been born."[7]

Of course others among the believers had their difficult moments as well. Following the Last Supper, Jesus left Peter, James, and John to wait while He ventured into the Garden of Gethsemane alone. When He fell on His face in prayer, "sorrowful . . . unto death,"[8] the record says, His sweat came as great drops of blood[9] as He pled with the Father to let this crushing, brutal cup pass from Him. But, of course, it could not pass. Returning from such anguished prayer, He found His three chief disciples asleep, prompting Him to ask, "Could ye not watch with me one hour?"[10] So it happens two more times, until on His third return He says compassionately, "Sleep on now, and take your rest,"[11] though there would be no rest for Him.

Later, after Jesus's arrest and appearance at trial, Peter, accused of knowing Jesus and being one of His confidants, denies that accusation not once but three times. We don't know all that was going on here, nor do we know of protective counsel that the Savior may have given to His Apostles privately,[12] but we do know Jesus was aware that even these precious ones would not stand with Him in the end, and He had warned Peter accordingly.[13] Then, with the crowing of the cock, "the Lord turned, and looked upon Peter. And Peter remembered the word of the Lord. . . . And [he] went out, and wept bitterly."[14]

Thus, of divine necessity, the supporting circle around Jesus gets smaller and smaller and smaller, giving significance to Matthew's words: "All the disciples [left] him, and fled."[15] Peter stayed near enough to be recognized and confronted. John stood at the foot of the cross with Jesus's mother. Especially and always the blessed women in the Savior's life stayed as close to Him as they could. But essentially His lonely journey back to His Father continued without comfort or companionship.

Now I speak very carefully, even reverently, of what may have been the most difficult moment in all of this solitary journey to Atonement. I speak of those final moments for which

Jesus must have been prepared intellectually and physically but which He may not have fully anticipated emotionally and spiritually—that concluding descent into the paralyzing despair of divine withdrawal when He cries in *ultimate* loneliness, "My God, my God, why hast *thou* forsaken me?"[16]

The loss of mortal support He had anticipated, but apparently He had not comprehended this. Had He not said to His disciples, "Behold, the hour . . . is now come, that ye shall be scattered, every man to his own, and shall leave me alone: and yet I am not alone, because the Father is with me" and "The Father hath not left me alone; for I do always those things that please him"?[17]

With all the conviction of my soul I testify that He *did* please His Father perfectly and that a perfect Father did *not* forsake His Son in that hour. Indeed, it is my personal belief that in all of Christ's mortal ministry the Father may never have been closer to His Son than in these agonizing final moments of suffering. Nevertheless, that the supreme sacrifice of His Son might be as complete as it was voluntary and solitary, the Father briefly withdrew from Jesus the comfort of His Spirit, the support of His personal presence. It was required, indeed it was central to the significance of the Atonement, that this perfect Son who had never spoken ill nor done wrong nor touched an unclean thing had to know how the rest of humankind—us, all of us—would feel when we did commit such sins. For His Atonement to be infinite and eternal, He had to feel what it was like to die not only physically but spiritually, to sense what it was like to have the divine Spirit withdraw, leaving one feeling totally, abjectly, hopelessly alone.

But Jesus held on. He pressed on. The goodness in Him allowed faith to triumph even in a state of complete anguish. The trust He lived by told Him in spite of His feelings that divine compassion is never absent, that God is always faithful, that He never flees nor fails us. When the uttermost farthing had then been paid, when Christ's determination to be faithful was as obvious as it was utterly invincible, finally and mercifully, it was "finished."[18] Against all odds and with none to help or uphold Him, Jesus of Nazareth, the living Son of the living God, restored physical life where death had held sway and brought joyful, spiritual redemption out of sin, hellish darkness, and despair. With faith in the God He *knew* was there, He could say in triumph, "Father, into thy hands I commend my spirit."[19]

One of the great consolations of our mortality is that because Jesus walked such a long, lonely path utterly alone, *we* do not have to do so. His solitary journey brought great company for our little version of that path—the merciful care of our Father in Heaven, the unfailing companionship of this Beloved Son, the consummate gift of the Holy Ghost, angels in heaven, family members on both sides of the veil, prophets and apostles, teachers, leaders, friends. All of these and more have been given as companions for our mortal journey because of the Atonement of Jesus Christ and the Restoration of His gospel. Trumpeted from the summit of Calvary is the truth that we will never be left alone nor unaided, even if sometimes we may feel that we are. Truly the Redeemer of us all said: "I will not leave you comfortless: [My Father and] I will come to you [and abide with you]."[20]

My plea is that these scenes of Christ's lonely sacrifice, laced with moments of denial and abandonment and, at least once, outright betrayal, must *never* be reenacted by us. He has walked alone once. Now, may I ask that never again will He have to confront sin without our aid and assistance, that never again will He find only unresponsive onlookers when He sees you and me along His *Via Dolorosa* in our present day. May we declare ourselves to be more fully disciples of the Lord Jesus Christ, not in word only and not only in the flush of comfortable times but in deed and in courage and in faith, including when the path is lonely and when our cross is difficult to bear. May we stand by Jesus Christ "at all times and in all things, and in all places that [we] may be in, even until death,"[21] for surely that is how He stood by us when it *was* unto death and when He had to stand entirely and utterly alone.

NOTES

From a talk given at general conference, April 2009.

1. Isaiah 63:3, 5; see also Doctrine and Covenants 76:107; 88:106; 133:50.
2. Matthew 26:65–66; see footnote 66b.
3. Luke 23:14.
4. Matthew 27:26.
5. See Bible Dictionary, "Barabbas," 619.
6. Matthew 27:21.
7. Matthew 26:24.

8. Matthew 26:38.

9. See Luke 22:44; Mosiah 3:7; Doctrine and Covenants 19:18.

10. Matthew 26:40.

11. Matthew 26:45.

12. See Spencer W. Kimball, "Peter, My Brother," in *Brigham Young University Speeches of the Year* (July 13, 1971), 5.

13. See Mark 14:27–31.

14. Luke 22:61–62.

15. Matthew 26:56.

16. Matthew 27:46; emphasis added.

17. John 16:32; 8:29.

18. See John 19:30.

19. Luke 23:46.

20. John 14:18; see also v. 23.

21. Mosiah 18:9.

Index

Smith, 213–15. *See also* Witness, standing as
Therapy, 190–91
Thoreau, Henry David, 196
Thoughts: controlling, 139; happiness and, 200–201
Tongues, Satan binds, of faithful, 86
Tree of Life vision, 212–13
Trials: of early Saints, 20–21; of Joseph Smith and early Saints, 35–39; as redemptive experiences, 39–41; as necessary, 41–42; as blessings and learning experiences, 42–43; inevitability of, 43–45; suffered by righteous, 45–48; charity during, 48–50; cheerfulness during, 50–51; in marriage, 70–72; righteousness through, 102; of missionary work, 113–14; of Elder and Sister Holland during early years of marriage, 151–52; of Adam and Eve, 163–64; of latter days, 165, 173–74; mental illness as, 187–93; of Lehi's family, 197; keeping covenants through, 225–26, 227
Trust, 67–68, 178–84, 228–31. *See also* Belief; Faith

Vengeance, 48–50
Virtue, 200

War, 173
Wayward Church members, 98–99, 102–7

"We Are All Enlisted," 86, 88–89, 90–91
Wilderness, Israelites sent into, 94–95
Will of God, submission to, 229–32
Winter's Tale, The (Shakespeare), 230
Witness, standing as, 100–102, 178–84. *See also* Testimony
Women: abuse of, 68; gratitude for, 156–57, 233; as disciples of Jesus Christ, 233–34; priesthood and, 235–39; husbands' duties toward, 240–41; discrimination against, 241–42; righteous, 242–43; as force for righteousness, 245. *See also* Motherhood
Wood, 158
Wordsworth, William, 66
Work, 203–7
Worthiness, for missionary work, 87–89
Worthy, suffering of, 45–47

"Ye Elders of Israel," 93
Young, Brigham: and migration of Latter-day Saints, 95–96; on righteousness, 182; on government of God, 239
Young, Bruce, 230–32
Young men, as army of Lord, 87–89
Youth: work of, 7; moral cleanliness and, 75–83

Zacharias, Ravi, 130–31
Zion, 94–97